★★★★★★★★★★★★★★★★★★

Abandoning Method

Sociological Studies in Methodology

★★★★★★★★★★★★★★★★★★

★★★★★★★★★★★★★★★★★★

Derek L. Phillips

★★★★★★★★★★★★★★★★★★

★★★★★★★★★★★★★★★★★★★★

ABANDONING METHOD

★★★★★★★★★★★★★★★★★★★★

Jossey-Bass Publishers
San Francisco · Washington · London · 1973

ABANDONING METHOD
Sociological Studies in Methodology
by Derek L. Phillips

Library of Congress Catalogue Card Number LC 72-13598

International Standard Book Number ISBN 0-87589-165-9

Manufactured in the United States of America

JACKET DESIGN BY WILLI BAUM

FIRST EDITION

Code 7307

★★★★★★★★★★★★★★★★

The Jossey-Bass
Behavioral Science Series

★★★★★★★★★★★★★★★★

This book is for my children
Kimberly, Brad, and Todd

★★★★★★★★★★★★★★★★

Preface

★★★★★★★★★★★★★★★★

Abandoning Method has two purposes. First, I want to bring to the attention of sociologists and other students of social life a series of empirical studies of bias and invalidity in sociological reasearch. Whereas most previous investigations have examined these factors in a post hoc manner so as to make sense of discrepant or unexpected findings, the studies presented in Part One were designed explicitly to investigate bias and invalidity in large-scale survey studies. The underlying rationale for these studies is clear: the enormous amount of attention given to constructing sociological theories about the "hows" and "whys" of various social facts and empirical relationships makes little sense if these so-called facts and relationships are spurious or nonexistent. Furthermore, if measurements of social phenomena are inadequate, even the most sophisticated and advanced procedures of data analysis will not yield explanations.

My second purpose, developed in Part Two, is to raise questions about much that is ignored or simply taken for granted in the studies reported in the first half of the book. These studies were conducted with the assumption that by discovering certain sources of bias and invalidity it would be possible to control for or eliminate them in future research, but in Part Two I question this assumption as well as other beliefs and worldviews underlying the practice of much sociology. Among other things, I examined how sociologists make decisions about what is or is not to be accepted as sociological knowledge. I then consider the usefulness of what Popper calls "falsification" and whether falsification can operate when different "paradigms" (Kuhn) are being compared. These issues exist in all sciences, although I give special attention to their sociological applications.

In the final chapters, I apply Wittgenstein's notion of "form of life" to sociology. I examine such sociological concepts as discovery, cause, bias, and objectivity—all of which are generally left unexamined by sociologists. Further, I begin to consider the importance of method as a necessary condition for the existence of any scientific community and try to show the consequences of this view for sociological inquiry. Also in these chapters, I point to the similarities between certain so-called new sociological approaches (symbolic-interactionism, ethnomethodology, and phenomenology) and the dominant approach to which they are supposedly alternatives.

Thus Parts One and Two are radically different, even though they share a common concern with issues of method and methodology. However, I must emphasize that *Abandoning Method* is not intended to show anyone the correct way to do sociology. On the contrary, much of what I have to say is explicitly opposed to the whole notion of "correct" method. It has become almost a cliche among an increasing number of sociologists that methodology is too important to be left to methodologists, and I certainly hold that point of view. In fact, all the essays in the second part of the book were written in reaction to those sociologists who create and maintain boundaries in the study of social life and who worry about whether something is "really" sociology.

The four chapters constituting Part One take up a series of basic themes developed in my earlier book, *Knowledge from What?* and they provide further empirical evidence for some of the conclusions advanced there. They were all written before I came to live and teach in the Netherlands in the late summer of 1971. Prior to the beginning of the academic year 1971–1972, I had a series of meetings with some of my new colleagues at the University of Amsterdam. As we discussed my plans for a graduate course in methodology, it quickly became evident that the majority of my colleagues were strongly opposed to my ideas for the course. While I intended to use some of the work of Winch, Cicourel, and others who were critical of much contemporary sociology, my colleagues argued that such selections were inappropriate and that what students "really needed" was a firmer grounding in statistics and various methods of data collection and analysis. Once students had acquired a firm foundation then perhaps in the last portion of the course such "extreme" views as mine might be presented. Actually my views were not so extreme, although my colleagues thought so. Some argued that mine was not really a course in methodology, and some even suggested that perhaps it was not even sociology! I was not really surprised to find that they did not share my views. But what I found totally unexpected was their apparent *certainty* about what was appropriate and proper sociological methodology and their further belief that such matters as course content (including the books to be used and the numbers of pages to be read) should be decided jointly by staff members and student representatives. Since my appointment was to the section of "Methods and Techniques," I was expected to be a good citizen (which I was not), and permit those advocating what I considered the traditional view of sociological methods to decide the content of my course—despite that fact that I had been offered a position at the University of Amsterdam partly, I thought, because of the dissenting views presented in *Knowledge from What?* and some of my other writings. Fortunately, we did manage to work things out satisfactorily. But this experience eventually led me to alter still further some of my views on methodology, as well as to give more serious attention to the matter of membership in a scientific community.

In an attempt to more clearly formulate my own position on some of the problems resulting from these discussions with my colleagues, I wrote and circulated an early draft of what is now Chapter Five of this book. My colleagues' reactions were enormously useful to me, not only because they served to highlight our points of disagreement but also because they enabled me to better realize how much my own views and persuasions had begun to change. The remaining chapters of *Abandoning Method* were also initially written in response to my colleagues' views on sociology and science. Although I do not know whether or not I had any influence on them, their criticisms and reactions to my views forced me to examine much that I had previously taken for granted or ignored. Thus I am extremely grateful to them, both for providing the impetus for the essays in Part Two and for their remarks and comments on earlier drafts.

My disagreements are not only with my colleagues here in the Netherlands, of course. Most of my former students and colleagues in the United States also do not seem to think there is anything intrinsically wrong with sociology as it now is. Rather they believe that we are just using it for the wrong purposes or for the wrong people, or that it is only a "young science" that has yet to reach maturity. Most appear perfectly willing to consider themselves as technical specialists or professionals. As I try to make clear in the final chapter, I do not share that viewpoint. I believe we must be extremely critical of sociological methods and theories. A critique of sociological methods is indispensable, both for the strengthening of the sociologist's self-awareness and for the reconstruction of sociology itself. Unless we turn our gaze upon ourselves and our work, we cannot realize the reconstruction of the societies in which we live.

The first five chapters of this book have appeared previously, in somewhat different form, in the *American Behavioral Scientist, American Sociological Review, American Journal of Sociology, Public Opinion Quarterly,* and *Mens en Maatschappij.* Kevin Clancy was my collaborator on Chapters Two, Three, and Four, and I appreciate his willingness to allow me to publish them here. We no longer share the same views about sociology and sociological inquiry, but I wish to thank him for his continued support and understanding. I also wish to thank my friend Eliot Freidson, who has tolerated and encouraged the various directions that my sociology has taken over the past several years. Most of all, I must express my special gratitude to Alan Blum and Alvin Gouldner who, in different ways, have been sources of inspiration and guidance. None of these friends will agree with what is said in this book, but it is written with them in mind.

Amsterdam
January 1973

DEREK L. PHILLIPS

★★★★★★★★★★★★★★★★

Contents

★★★★★★★★★★★★★★★★

★★★★★★★★★★★★★★★★★★

Abandoning Method

Sociological Studies in Methodology

★★★★★★★★★★★★★★★★★★

The word methodology
has a double meaning.
Not only a physical investigation
but also a conceptual one can be called
"methodological investigation."

LUDWIG WITTGENSTEIN

★★★★★★★★★★★★★★★★★★★★

1

Sociologists and Their Knowledge

★★★★★★★★★★★★★★★★★★★★

Sociology is becoming increasingly popular and respectable as an established field of study for college students. Even high school students are being introduced to it. This proliferation of sociology is assumed to be a good thing, at least insofar as it helps to develop the quality of mind that C. Wright Mills (1959, p. 7) terms "the sociological imagination": "the capacity to shift from one perspective to another—from the political to the psychological; from examination of a single family to comparative assessment of the national budgets of the world; from the theological school to the military establishment; from considerations of an oil industry to studies of contemporary poetry."[1]

[1] Mills acknowledged that the term "sociological imagination" could easily be replaced by the term "anthropological" or "political" imagination, or some other term, and that he was not speaking merely of the academic

But it is not only students who are increasingly receptive to sociologists and sociological thought, for sociology is seen by many as making significant contributions to other sectors of society as well. As is noted by Smelser and Davis (1969, pp. 116–117): "Sociologists are being hired in greater numbers by government agencies, businesses, hospitals, and other organizations. They are summoned more frequently on vital public issues. And they find themselves quoted more often in the public media as experts on one issue or another." Horowitz (1968, p. 262) observes that the social sciences "have in recent times begun to play a new and problematic role with respect to national and international policy. The problem of social policy has become acute precisely to the extent to which social science has become exact." Sociologists not only are employed by governmental and other organizations in increasing numbers but also serve on presidential commissions (such as the President's Advisory Commission on Civil Disorders) and in other high advisory posts. Obviously, these agencies assume that the sociologist has something important to contribute. Lazarsfeld and his associates in their book *The Uses of Sociology* (1967, pp. x–xi) state the following:

The sociologist can play a variety of roles in relation to the client: he can share whatever general wisdom he has acquired; he can do a special study; he can sensitize personnel to sociological orientations. Sometimes he will assume the stance of general social critic. The sociologist has at his disposal a variety of "resources." He has developed concepts and empirical generalizations, and sometimes theories. His techniques and experience are needed for specific studies—custom-tailored to the problem at hand. Finally, like all experts, he has encountered other situations seemingly very different from those in which the client finds himself which provide unexpected analogies—a major way to broaden the range of alternatives policy-makers perceive.

The sociologist, rather than being viewed as a cloistered scholar, is

---

discipline of sociology. Therefore, it seems that many claims made for sociology by such writers as Bierstedt (1964) are excessive and misleading. Bressler (1967) has made a similar criticism.

now seen as a professional, an expert whose knowledge and advice are considered sufficiently valuable to be worth soliciting and applying to contemporary social issues.

However, sociologists differ among themselves on the question of the application of sociological knowledge. Some are hostile or indifferent to applying the field to policy issues; others feel that sociology should be used to benefit one or another group in society; still others argue that sociologists should speak out as "experts" whether or not they are involved in a specific consulting or advisory capacity. A host of recent articles raise questions about the relevance of sociology, its impact on the society, value-free sociology, and issues of partisanship (see, for example, Becker, 1967; Gouldner, 1962, 1968, 1970; Tumin, 1968; and two excellent collections of papers, Douglas, 1970a, 1970b). Whatever side one takes on these issues, it seems perfectly obvious to me that sociologists will become more and more involved in trying to solve a great variety of societal problems. And they will occupy positions of increasing influence as they continue to gain access to the corridors of power in American society.

Role of Sociology

No matter what their position on the uses of sociology, almost all sociologists seem to assume that the profession possesses a unique and valuable body of "knowledge" or expertise. The quarrels and divisions in the field do not center around knowledge but rather around whether or not this knowledge should be put to work, and if so, for whom. At the 1968 meetings of the American Sociological Association, Martin Nicolaus, a member of the Sociology Liberation Movement, addressed some highly critical remarks to the assembled audience. He describes the sociological researcher as a "kind of spy" and observes (Nicolaus, 1969, p. 155), "The more adventurous sociologists don the disguise of the people and go out to mix with the peasants in the 'field,' returning with the books and articles that break the protective secrecy in which a subjugated population wraps itself, and make it more accessible to manipulation and control." Nicolaus accuses sociologists of taking knowledge from the people and giving it to the rulers. He (1969, p. 155) continues: "What if the machinery were reversed? What if the habits, problems, actions, and decisions of the wealthy and powerful were daily scrutinized by a thousand systematic researchers, were hourly pried into, analyzed, and cross-referenced, tabulated, and published in a hundred mass-circulated journals and written so that even the fifteen-year-old high school drop-out could understand it and predict the actions of their [sic] parents' landlord, manipulate and control 'him'?"

I have no strong quarrel with Nicolaus' assertions that sociologists are the servants of the power structure, for I generally share that view. But I do differ with him in regard to his belief that sociologists actually know something important that could be used to the advantage of those in power and against what he calls the "occupied populace." That is, it is one thing to argue that sociologists (knowingly or unknowingly) serve to legitimate the decisions of some power elite and quite another to argue that they use knowledge which actually enhances that power. I would not have expected a young radical sociologist to share with the sociological elite the belief that sociologists possess some unique body of knowledge that can be put to the use of one or another segment of the society. Reflecting on Nicolaus' remarks, however, I have come to realize that his assumption is shared by numerous other sociologists in the radical tradition: for example, C. Wright Mills, Alvin Gouldner, Irving Louis Horowitz, and Robert Lynd. In 1939, more than thirty years ago, Lynd in his famous *Knowledge for What?* chastised his fellow social scientists for their unwillingness to utilize their "knowledge" for the betterment of mankind. He argued that in many instances social scientists already possessed the knowledge necessary to bring about certain societal benefits. Considering the matter of war, for example, Lynd (1964, p. 241) asserted that "the causes of war are known and accepted by a wide group of thoughtful students." And Lynd felt that there were other areas of societal concern in which the social scientist had a special expertise.

A few writers have questioned the majority belief that the efficacy of sociology is already established. For instance, while most discussions of Project Camelot revolved around the propriety of the project, there were some who doubted the existence or creation of a body of sociological knowledge. Horowitz (1968, p. 298) points out that "no public document or statement contested the possibility that, given a successful completion of the data-gathering, Camelot could have, indeed, established basic criteria for measuring the level and potential for internal war in a given nation." And Tilly (1966) notes that the project was "in a field in which the most recent symposium—Harry Eckstein's *Internal War*—had displayed almost no established uniformities and no agreement whatsoever on theory, method, or likely hypotheses."

Clearly, it is not unreasonable to question how good sociological knowledge actually is. But what is the meaning of the term *knowledge?*

In considering this question, I find myself in agreement with Meehan (1968, p. 15), who notes that: "At the most fundamental level, knowledge is organized experience and the search for knowledge is a search for patterns of organization." The knowledge possessed by one or another social science consists of the organized experiences of men that have been assembled or accumulated so that they are publicly available. In this sense, all of the social sciences possess knowledge. The only way sociologists can evaluate the adequacy of their knowledge is in terms of how useful it is for a specific purpose. The social sciences consider that the major purpose of knowledge is to provide *explanations* of various social phenomena. Judgments concerning the adequacy of knowledge possessed by sociologists consequently have to be made on the basis of their abilities to explain the social phenomena that concern them. Although there is no firm consensus about exactly what *explanation* means, it is possible to describe some of the ways sociologists use it.

Accuracy of Data

Many explanations are evaluated in terms of their providing new information or new insights about various events and situations, descriptions of what happened, or understanding regarding the relations among various social phenomena. Sociologists attempt to "account" for an event or other social phenomenon so as to provide a conceptual scheme or framework in which the phenomenon is "plausible" or "makes sense." A problem with such criteria is that we do not have any agreed on bases for judging whether various investigators have accomplished their goals. For instance, how do we determine whether an explanation is insightful or plausible? How do we determine whether studies provide "good" explanations?

Consider, for instance, the controversies surrounding Lewis' (1951) replication of Redfield's (1930) Tepoztlan study. Whereas Redfield, in his conclusions, stressed the extent of integration in the community, Lewis emphasized the strains and tensions. What, then, do we "know" about Tepoztlan? Whose explanation of life in the community do we accept? And on what basis do we decide? Or consider Riesman's *The Lonely Crowd* (1950) and the criticisms of his conclusions by other social scientists (Lipset and Lowenthal, 1961). Clearly, what constitutes a plausible explanation for one social scientist may not be persuasive to some of his brethren. The lack of agreed on criteria makes it difficult to judge the adequacy of explanations of this type.

However, we are in a somewhat better position to evaluate those who emphasize both *explanation* (in a particular sense) and *prediction*. For instance, Smelser (1969, pp. 13–14) asserts that "explanation . . . begins with the search for independent variables (or causes, or determinants, or factors, or conditions) to which variations in the dependent variables are referred." And Coleman (1969, p. 107) states that "one of the important fruits of sociological investigations should be its ability to predict." One way to ascertain whether those stressing explanation and prediction have accomplished their goals is to consider the amount of *variance* in their dependent variables which can be accounted for by their principle independent variables. The aim, of course, is to find a relatively small number of variables that will explain the variation in many other variables. The variance in one variable is said to be explained by another to the extent that the variables covary or correlate. Yet the evidence concerning the extent to which certain sociological variables are able to explain the variations in other variables is rather unimpressive. For example, L. K. Miller (cited in Hamblin, 1966) examined the results of all studies published in the first three issues of the *American Sociological Review* in 1961 and found that the average "significant" relationship explained about 10 percent of the variance. Psychologists have been similarly unsuccessful in their attempts to account for much variance. For instance, Rosenthal (1966, p. 110) estimates that most behavioral research accounts for something like 13 percent of the variance of independent variables. Clearly, an ability to account for only 10 or 13 or even 20 percent of the variance is not very impressive and does not lead to a high degree of predictive ability. (Dunnette, 1966, has reached a similar conclusion with regard to explained variance in psychological investigations.)

Given the difficulties and problems concerning sociological explanations, what can be said about the generalizations which many social scientists regard as the highest product of their inquiries? Although many seem reluctant to admit it, we seem, in fact, to have been unable to provide generalizations that explain very much of the social behavior in which we are interested. Although hundreds, if not thousands, of generalizations abound in the literature, the vast number either are unconfirmed in empirical research or are of such minor magnitude in explaining any observable facts as to be of little utility. Psychologist Sears (1951, p. 466) notes that "an appallingly small number of the relationships that have been discovered in social psychology can be generalized. . . . With respect to attitude measurement, for example, one might ask whether *any* general principles of an antecedent-consequent nature have been found." And sociologist Whyte (1969, p. 22) relates that "years ago the late Louis Wirth used to terrify Ph.D. candidates by requiring them to name *one* proposition that had been reasonably well-supported by research data." In my view, contemporary sociologists (and, I suspect, most social scientists) would be as hard-pressed as Wirth's students.

While there are many reasons for this state of affairs, one way to consider them is to look more closely at what constitutes an explanation. Sociologists speak of having explained something when they have provided descriptions, insights, plausible interpretations, when they have established correlations or empirical interrelationships, or when they are able to successfully predict. Although the issues surrounding explanation are far too complex to be dealt with adequately here,[2] I think it is useful to offer some further thoughts on explanations in sociology.

[2] Some of these issues are considered at length in the results of a

Clearly, a description of the phenomenon being investigated is a necessary part of any explanation; we need to know *what* happened, what are the facts to be explained. In addition to the description (the what), we require an interpretation of it; we need to know *why* it happens or occurs. We need to account for or make sense of the phenomenon. Some sociologists argue that they have accomplished an interpretation when they can provide a set of general statements or some conceptual framework from which one can generate, or to which one can relate, a correlation or other description. Unfortunately, there is a good deal of vagueness in the sociological literature as to what is meant by a "conceptual framework" or a "set of general statements."

When description and interpretation are combined, we have what some regard as a "complete explanation" (DiRenzo, 1966). Obviously not all sociologists are explicitly concerned with both aspects. In fact the great majority are concerned with either the whats or the whys. Many are concerned primarily with establishing the "facts"—descriptions of various social phenomena. This is essentially the goal of many who engage in empirical research. Although the researcher often does attempt to provide fuller explanations for some facts, frequently the whys are left to those who call themselves theorists. Clearly, however, both the researcher and the theorist require that the facts to be explained (the whats) are in good order. Whether a sociologist is interested in consumer attitudes, seasonal variations in cotton prices in various parts of the world, socialization processes, the workings of the Supreme Court, the relationship between educational level and voting preferences, patterns of religious behavior, or the ideological origins of American thought, he is dependent on the adequacy of his data. Whether the data come from interviews, questionnaires, observations, records, documents, archival materials, or whatever, the sociologist must assure that his evidence is valid. Should there be serious questions about the facts to be explained, there is little reason for trying to determine how or why they came about. Therefore a necessary but in-

---

symposium on the theme "Conceptual Definitions in the Behavioral Sciences," which has been published as a collection of essays edited by DiRenzo (1966).

sufficient condition for a complete explanation is that the facts be established.

Many sociologists assume that the facts have been determined and that what we need to do is account for the whys. In my view, however, the accuracy of the facts to be explained is often subject to considerable question. For example, Price asserts that "facts are empirically verifiable statements about social phenomena. For example, it is a fact that the suicide rate in the United States in 1962 was 10.8 per 100,000 population" (1969, p. iv). If we accept Price's assertion that this is a fact, then we might want to move on to speculate (or discover) why this rate is higher or lower than the rate in some other country. But is it a fact? I think not, for as Douglas (1967), among others, has so clearly shown, the "operational definition" of a suicide differs both among and within societies. The bureaucratic officials determine who is classified as a suicide, and they do so in various ways. A recent television newscast in New York City noted that 1,100 persons in the city died within the last year as a result of "suicides." Who made the decision on suicides, on what basis, for what reasons? Need the deceased have left a note, appeared depressed, or what? Because there is considerable reason to be skeptical about Price's fact, the spinning of theories to explain it may be an exercise in futility.

Consider two other areas where attempts have been made to validate the facts (as indicated by people's responses to interviews) by examining information contained in various records: voting studies and studies of health and illness. Bell and Buchanan (1956) found that 30 percent of respondents in a "general population" gave inaccurate replies to a question on voting; Parry and Crossley (1950) found that 23 percent of their respondents said they had voted when they actually had not done so; and Cahalan (1968) reports that 28 percent of Denver respondents exaggerated their vote in the 1947 mayoralty election. A study by Cannell and Fowler (1963), concerned with the accuracy of health information, revealed considerable discrepancies between people's reports to interviewers and the hospital records: 58 percent of respondents gave inaccurate reports concerning their length of stay in the hospital, 23 percent were inaccurate with regard to the month of discharge,

35 percent with regard to diagnosis, 25 percent with regard to type of surgery, and 10 percent were inaccurate in their reports as to whether surgery had even been performed.

Another type of sociological knowledge based on people's reports of their behavior is birth control information and usage. Numerous surveys have tried to ascertain "the facts" about use of various contraceptive devices. People's responses to inquiries about their use have generally been assumed to be valid, and widespread generalizations have been made on this basis. Recently, however, Green (1969) reported an investigation of the validity of the responses given as compared with the clinic records on the actual behavior of respondents regarding the use and knowledge of contraceptives in East Pakistan. The data included both information from the clinic and education program records and the verbal reports of behavior from respondents. It was found that people underreported both their use and knowledge of contraceptives (as determined by the records), although they were less reluctant to admit knowledge of family planning methods than they were to admit they used them. About one out of five men and one out of four women who (according to the records) knew of contraceptives denied knowledge of them. Of all couples who had used contraceptives (again, according to the records), about one out of every five husbands and one out of every three wives denied ever having used them. (For a more complete review of these studies see Phillips, 1971.)

Since the bulk of sociological data used for analyzing "causes" comes from interviews and questionnaires, unrecognized inaccuracies become part of the basic facts on which explanation is based. Consider a possibly more widespread source of inaccuracy, the United States Census—a source of data for a large number of sociologists. Cannell and Kahn (1968, p. 527) remark on the Census as follows:

Perhaps the prototypical example of research interviews is provided by the national census. Most countries of the world conduct some kind of population count, and in many countries the census has been expanded to provide with regularity an inventory of social resources and problems. Census interviews usually make only modest demands on interviewer and respondent. They are

> *brief; they ask for* demographic data well within the respondent's knowledge and not of a kind which he is likely to regard as confidential. *Moreover, the information is requested under circumstances familiar to or expected by most respondents, and the request is backed by the legitimate power of the national government* [*italics added*].

According to Cannell and Kahn, then, census data secured through research interviews are obtained under almost idyllic conditions.

Though there is little evidence on the extent of accuracy in census reports, two recent studies do shed considerable light on this matter. Hambright (1969) reports on an investigation where a sample of death certificates was matched with the 1960 census reports, thus allowing for a comparison of response data for items asked on both records. The data on the two reports were compared for the same persons, with inconsistencies between the two resulting from errors on either death or census records, although there was no way of determining where the errors lay. Hambright (p. 419) found a very low extent (less than 3 percent) of "disagreement" with regard to race and nativity. But for age and marital status, the disagreement was more considerable. Even when people's ages were compared in terms of ten-year intervals (p. 417), there was disagreement for 8.1 percent of white males and 11.4 percent of white females, and 23.8 percent for Negro males and 30.3 percent for Negro females. Disagreements for marital status were even greater in magnitude. For instance, the two sets of records failed to coincide in terms of the "single" status of 9.0 percent of white respondents and 21.6 percent of Negro respondents. For the category "divorced," the records were in disagreement with the reports of 26.5 percent of whites and 42.4 percent of Negroes.

A recent study by the Census Bureau itself (U. S. Bureau of the Census, 1965) compares occupational data obtained from respondents with that obtained from employers. Although only eight occupational groupings were used, 18 percent of all persons classified by the 1960 census in a given occupational group "really" belonged to another one. Commenting on these findings, Lebergott (1968) estimates that perhaps one-third of all persons were reported in the wrong occupation by the U. S. Census. It seems obvious, then, that reports concerning data "well within the respondent's knowledge and not of a kind which he is likely to regard as confidential" are subject to considerable inaccuracy.[3] This being the case, we would not be surprised to find extreme inaccuracies in reports of other social phenomena.

If inaccuracies in people's verbal reports (or any other sources of data) are disproportionately distributed in certain segments or subgroups of the population, the validity of certain relationships between the social scientist's independent and dependent variables is questionable. Not only are there inaccuracies with regard to voting, health care utilization, and the like, but these may be related to the independent variables which are used to explain certain facts. An example is the often-demonstrated inverse relationship between social-class position and F-scale authoritarianism, anomie, and prejudice (for example, McDill, 1961, Roberts and Rokeach, 1956, Srole, 1956). That is, authoritarianism, anomie, and prejudice are found to be more characteristic of the lower than of the upper classes. Christie (1954) suggests that the apparent social-class differences in authoritarianism may be due to intelligence or acquiescence rather than to actual differences in social class. And Kirscht and Dillehay (1967, pp. 38–39) have noted that many studies "included potential response biases as most items were worded so that agreement indicated intolerance, anomie, or the other variables tested. Probably some of the responses were due to the tendency of relatively unsophisticated subjects to respond favorably to 'high-sounding aphorisms.' " It also seems likely that more sophisticated respondents may be less likely to endorse items such as those on the F-scale. (See also Miller and Riessman, 1961.) Similar factors affect studies of prejudice. Stember (1961, p. 170)

[3] An alternative explanation for the Hambright study is that those supplying information about the deceased (next of kin and friends) simply do not know the details of marriage and age concerning people close to them. This probably accounts for some of the discrepancies in the two reports, although I would think these others would have been as familiar with the marital status of the deceased as with their nativity. But even the idea that those supplying the information do not know people's ages and details of marriage has implications for some sociological research, especially that concerned with "proxy" reports by certain individuals regarding details about the characteristics and behavior of other family members (as is the case, of course, in the U. S. Census).

points out that items which are crude in nature may bypass the educated, and perhaps this is why "results of questions expressing extreme positions . . . have so often indicated a negative relationship between prejudice and education. When the issues are posed in more neutral terminology, no such relationship is evidenced."

Some of the same problems of response bias exist in the study of mental illness (which Szasz and others would say does not even exist as something to be explained) as it relates to social class. Clancy and I (see following chapter) present some evidence that the association between scores on a mental health inventory and social-class position may be due partially to the class-linked influence of another kind of response set—social desirability. My point here is that the discovery of an inverse relationship between social class and authoritarianism, anomie, prejudice, or mental illness can be taken at face value only if the measures of these variables (and the results of the measurement process) are reasonably valid. If, as appears possible, these various social phenomena are not really class-related, why spend time inventing one or another explanation to deal with how and why these (perhaps spurious) relationships came about? In my view, sociologists spend a disproportionate amount of time and energy trying to account for what may be nonexistent "facts" and nonexistent relationships.

But what if it were possible to establish with only a small degree of error the validity of our measures? What if the facts are beyond dispute? Are we then on more solid ground? Certainly we are in a better position to proceed, but even here the problems are formidable. Imagine that we have valid measures of our independent and dependent variables and that, furthermore, we have established an extremely high (statistical) relationship between them. This relationship does not in itself constitute an explanation. Rather a correlation is also a description—a fact to be explained. The fact itself does not serve as an explanation of anything at all. Thus, even if we have valid measures and strong associations between our variables (neither of which exists at present), the sociologist is still faced with the problem of making sense of or accounting for these facts. The nature of his interpretation will be determined by his own (frequently hidden) models of man, experiences in society, interests, persuasions, and so on. Given this state of affairs, there might be almost as many different interpretations of some demonstrated relationships as there are sociological orientations (or even sociologists). How, then, can we choose among varying interpretations even when we have the facts straight? Clearly, this is a difficult problem but one we must face and one to which some sociologists (such as Doby, 1969) have addressed themselves.[4]

Implications

What I have been arguing is that much of the evidence used by sociologists is of questionable validity; that, furthermore, the relationships between our chief independent and dependent variables are generally quite weak; and, finally, that even if we had valid measures and strong relationships the problems of interpretation are formidable. Although I may have overstated my case, let me suggest only two implications of my remarks—which, I believe, follow even if I am only partially correct.

First of all, we may be passing on to our students and colleagues a great deal of misinformation (as in the example of Price's fact concerning suicide) if our measures lack validity. Recently, both Blalock and Hauser have remarked on measurement problems in sociology. Blalock (1969, p. 115) observes that "certain kinds of inadequacies in our measurement procedures may very well provide the major obstacle to be overcome if sociology is to mature in the direction of becoming a 'hard' and disciplined social science." And Hauser asserts that the problem of adequate measurement is *the* major block to progress in sociological research. Speaking specifically of survey data, Hauser (1969, p. 127) states: "I believe that it is at least a moot point as to whether, up to this point in the use of survey results, more misinformation than information has been gathered on many subjects." I share Hauser's view and would generalize it to other modes of data collection. Thus, we may be unwittingly generating a good deal of misinformation which eventually finds its way into the hundreds of research reports and dozens of monographs and textbooks which are forthcoming yearly from members of the profession.

Secondly, and perhaps ultimately more important to the

[4] I have tried to deal with these issues elsewhere (Phillips, 1971).

lives of all of us, this misinformation with regard to the "what" of social life may serve to create certain social realities which, as we all know, may be real in their consequences. I offer an example taken from some remarks of Rosenberg (1967, p. 152): "There is now good reason to believe that a major contaminant operates in polls on matters of foreign policy. Many respondents who are essentially apathetic on foreign policy issues, who lack awareness of the very existence of some of these issues, may well characterize themselves invalidly when asked how they regard, say, the admission of Communist China into the U. N., wheat shipments to the Soviet Union, scientific cooperation with the Soviet Union, or even resumption of diplomatic relations with Cuba. More precisely, they are prone to report themselves as far more resistant than they actually are toward the mounting and execution of such conciliatory policies." If, as Rosenberg suggests, public opinion polls show people to be more "hard-line" than they actually are, and if, as there is good reason to believe, the policy elite takes public opinion poll results into account when they formulate foreign policy, then such misinformation may have the very real consequence of leading to even harder line positions on the part of the government. And this relationship does not end here, because there is continuing interplay between public opinion and policy decisions.

Misinformation may also result in what some of us regard as positive consequences.[5] For example, there may be a social desirability response bias operating in opinion polls pertaining to racial prejudice, so that people report themselves as far less resistant to certain changes in legislation pertaining to racial equality than they actually are. And some laws are changed because of such misinformation, as may have been the case in the North in recent years. After all, social norms operate in survey and public opinion polls as well as in the rest of society. There may be deflection of self-characterizing attitude reports (and consequent invalidity) toward a perceived consensus. With regard to issues of foreign policy, Rosenberg (1967, pp. 152–153) suggests that such deflection may be "fostered by such varied factors as uncertainty and anxiety over the possibility

[5] The best-known instance where this may have occurred is the Supreme Court's decision in *Brown v. Board of Education*. See, for instance, Garfinkel (1970).

that the public opinion interview is some kind of disguised test of loyalty [and] embarrassment that one's basic apathy toward foreign issues will earn the interviewer's disapproval."[6]

Let me acknowledge that much of this discussion is conjectural and problematic, but no more so than some of the social phenomena which many sociologists regard as "facts" to be explained. Certainly I do not mean to suggest that sociologists (or other social scientists) should stop work and close up shop. What I am arguing is that perhaps we should devote a good deal less attention to issues of how and for whom we should apply our knowledge and give greater recognition to the importance of distinguishing the various shades and levels involved in our knowledge. At present, there is much that passes for knowledge in the rhetoric of sociology, and frequently this so-called knowledge is used by privileged elites, and sometimes by radicals, to provide a facade of rationality for their actions. (And as Freidson, 1970, has clearly pointed out, medicine and other "professions" are subject to the same charge.) We must direct our skepticism inward as well as toward those whom we study. Berger (1963) and others have suggested that the first wisdom of sociology is that "things are not what they seem." I suggest that this may be as true for the discipline of sociology as for the rest of the world which we take as our subject matter. It is our responsibility as sociologists to acknowledge that, like others, there is much we do not know about the social world.

[6] Another paper by Rosenberg (1965) considers several different processes that may be involved in moving individuals toward false or exaggerated self-reports. Also, see Phillips (1971).

★★★★★★★★★★★★★★★★

2

Response Biases: Conditions and Consequences

★★★★★★★★★★★★★★★★

Having reviewed some of the literature concerning bias and invalidity in sociological investigations, I now turn to a discussion of my own studies of bias in empirical research. I begin with an area of inquiry which has received an enormous amount of time, effort, and funds: the study of mental illness.

Social scientists have long been concerned with determining the relationship of mental illness to various social factors, such as sex, age, race, occupation, educational level, and social class background. Most studies of the incidence (first admissions over a time period) and prevalence (total patients at a given point in time) of mental disorder have been based on treatment rates for various segments of the population. These investigations have revealed some rather consistent patterns of relationship between mental illness—including both neuroses and psychoses (especially schizophrenia)—and different social factors. (See, for example, Clark, 1948; Clausen and Kohn, 1959; Dunham, 1965; Frumkin, 1952; Hollingshead and Redlich, 1958; Kaplan and others, 1956; Pasamanick and others, 1959; and Wanklin and others, 1955.) However, it is becoming increasingly apparent that figures based on treatment rates provide an unsatisfactory estimate of the "true" incidence and true prevalence of mental illness, since treated disorder may not accurately reflect the total distribution of mental disorder in American society. Incidence rates reflect, among other things, the influence of short-term changes in the social structure (such as disasters and family strife), while prevalence rates are influenced by such considerations as the availability of psychiatric facilities and public attitudes toward those who use them.

Recognition of these problems has led to investigations of untreated as well as treated mental illness. Although there have been a few studies of "true incidence" (for example, Kaplan and others, 1956), the majority of investigations have tried to discover the "true prevalence" of mental disorder. Numerous studies using field interviews and questionnaires have attempted to estimate the existence of mental illness, especially neuroses. They found that mental illness is far more prevalent than it appears to be from analysis of treatment records. They also show recurrent patterns regarding the relationship of mental illness to different social-structural and social-psychological variables.

Despite heavy reliance on interviews and questionnaires in these studies, few attempts have been made to ascertain whether various response styles might be influencing some of these patterns and relationships.

In spite of the general lack of specific attention to response styles, two recent studies (Dohrenwend, 1966; Phillips and Segal, 1969) do focus on this problem. Specifically, they deal with Langner's 22-Item Mental Health Inventory—an inventory which has been used widely in studies of mental illness such as Abramson, 1966; Bailey and others, 1965; Dohrenwend, 1966; Dohrenwend and Crandell, 1967; Haberman, 1963; Langner, 1962, 1965, pp.

360–392; Manis and others, 1963, 1964; Martin, 1968; Meile and Haese, 1969; Phillips, 1966; Phillips and Segal, 1969.

This index consists of psychological, psychophysiological, and physiological indicators of mental disorder (Dohrenwend and Crandell, 1967; Langner, 1962). It asks respondents whether they are troubled by any of twenty-two symptoms of distress. Sample items are: "Do you feel somewhat apart or alone even among friends?"; "Do you have personal worries that get you down physically?"; "Do you ever have trouble in getting to sleep or staying asleep?" Respondents are then scaled from 0 to 22, depending on how many symptoms they admit to. Langner (1962) reports that a score of 4 or more indicates psychiatric impairment. He states that in the Midtown Study, among people classified as "well" (no significant impairment) by Midtown psychiatrists, only 1 percent had scores of 4 or more; while among those classified as "incapacitated" (serious symptoms with total impairment), 84 percent had a score of 4 or more. Most investigators using this inventory have followed Langner and used a score of 4 as the cut-off point in their studies of psychiatric disorder.

Phillips and Segal use Langner's inventory to examine the relationship between sexual status and psychiatric symptoms. They hypothesize that women report more psychiatric symptoms than men with the same number of physical illnesses. Their argument is simply that it is culturally more appropriate and acceptable in American society for women to be expressive about their difficulties and, therefore, that they are more likely than men to *report* or *admit to* certain acts, behaviors, and feelings that lead to their being categorized as mentally ill. While their findings support this argument, the study has one obvious limitation: it lacks a measure of what men and women see as appropriate or "socially desirable" behavior for someone of their sexual status.

The study by Dohrenwend deals more adequately with this problem. In questioning the validity of Langner's index and other symptom inventories used in some mental health studies, Dohrenwend suggests that response biases may play an important role in determining the replies (and hence, the rates) obtained in these investigations. Since such biases, or stylistic variables, reduce the validity of measuring instruments, their possible effects should be understood and, if possible, accounted for. Dohrenwend considers what are possibly the two most often studied response styles in the literature: social desirability and acquiescence. Social desirability describes the tendency of people to deny socially undesirable traits and to "admit" socially desirable ones. According to Edwards (1959, pp. 101–116), much of the variance in all self-inventories of personality can be explained by this factor. Acquiescence, in contrast, denotes the tendency to agree (or disagree) with items independent of their content. This tendency is sometimes referred to as "yeasaying" or (for disagreement) "naysaying" (Couch and Keniston, 1960).

Because these two styles of answering questions may be related to survey responses and because they are perhaps differentiated among various groups (by age, sex, or socioeconomic, ethnic, or racial status), field studies of mental illness may be more reflective of differential propensities toward certain response styles than of psychiatric disorder. Numerous studies, for example, demonstrate an inverse relationship between mental illness and social class position (see Dohrenwend, 1966; Gurin and others, 1960; Hollingshead and Redlich, 1958; Phillips, 1966; Srole and others, 1962), and some of them use the Langner index. Yet Dohrenwend offers preliminary evidence that both people's assessments of the desirability of Langner's symptom items and tendencies to yeasay are inversely related to class. If there is, indeed, a strong relationship between response styles and replies to the inventory, and if propensities toward response styles are *not* randomly distributed among respondents in different social strata, then field studies of mental illness clearly have validity problems.

Social Desirability

Dohrenwend found that most people saw the characteristics called for by the items in Langner's inventory as somewhat undesirable. He indicates (1966, p. 23) that on a 9-point desirability scale (1 representing extremely undesirable, and 9 representing extremely desirable), the average rating given the twenty-two items was 3.2. Thus people who score "high" on undesirability may tend to suppress admission of those symptoms they judge socially undesirable. This tendency would not vitiate comparisons among strata were the evaluation of the desirability of the items constant across the different social strata. However, Dohrenwend provides some evidence that constancy is not the case. For example, Puerto Ricans in his sample perceived the twenty-two items as more desirable than did respondents of Irish and Jewish backgrounds (p. 24). We would expect to find, therefore, a higher prevalence of psychiatric impairment as measured by the twenty-two-item inventory among Puerto Ricans than among the Irish and Jews. This expectation is realized in his data. (However, Dohrenwend is guilty of the "ecological" or "aggregate" fallacy. He, in effect, looked at correlations between the characteristics of groups of people and then drew conclusions regarding correlations between individuals.)

An important question here is the relationship between ethnicity and the evaluation of the desirability of the twenty-two items. Why do Puerto Ricans perceive the items as more desirable than do other groups? Dohrenwend posits two alternative hypotheses. Following a line of thinking outlined by Heilbrun (1964), he writes that the Puerto Ricans in his Washington Heights sample (p. 24) "regard the characteristics described in the 22-item screening instrument as less undesirable than do members of other groups. It seems possible that they would also be more willing than other groups, on this account, to admit such characteristics. If so, they may actually have a much lower rate of disorder than their rate of reported symptoms would suggest. On the other hand, the reason Puerto Ricans see these symptoms as less undesirable may be because they are actually more common among Puerto Ricans. If this is so, then higher rates of reported symptoms among Puerto Ricans and their lower tendency to see these symptoms as strongly undesirable may both indicate the same thing—higher actual rates of disorder."

The second of Dohrenwend's hypotheses suggests that an individual comes to learn or perceive the desirability of a given symptom by observing the prevalence of that symptom among people like himself, other people of his ethnic or socioeconomic background. This might be termed a traditional, reference-group interpretation. Dohrenwend argues that if symptoms are common among one's own status group—in this case, family, friends, and neighbors—the desirability of the items will be higher than if the symptoms are not common.

This interpretation suggests that the social environment of an individual determines his evaluations as to the desirability of given symptoms and that the most important aspect of this social environment is the actual prevalence of these symptoms among his friends and acquaintances. This may or may not be the case. In our society, for example, it is a common observation that many persons have aquiline noses. Let an aquiline nose represent a symptom. Then according to Dohrenwend, aquiline noses should be considered desirable by those persons who have them. Obviously, this line of reasoning does not account for the vogue among many women (and some men, as well) with aquiline noses to have a "nose job." Similarly, this line of thought does not account for the efforts some Negroes make to "pass," the striving of the Irish, Germans, Italians, Jews, and now, Puerto Ricans, to lose their native "accent," or for other similar everyday instances where members of a given group seem to consider characteristics highly common within that group (but less common in the larger society) to be undesirable.

If we assume for the moment, though, that Dohrenwend is correct, and if we assume that both variables relate to an individual's score on a mental health inventory, then we would expect a desirability measure and some measure of the symptom prevalence among the respondent's acquaintances to be highly correlated and thus to be redundant predictors of an individual's mental health score. In a multiple regression analysis, for example, we would anticipate that the addition of a measure of symptom prevalence among people's acquaintance groups would not significantly increase the ability of a desirability measure to predict a mental health score, because both independent variables would be highly correlated (redundant). Hence, a test of this hypothesis would be to determine whether item desirability and estimated prevalence of psychiatric symptoms are in fact independent or redundant predictors of mental health scores. If this hypothesis were supported, we would no longer need to concern ourselves with possible desirability bias in replies to the 22-Item Mental Health Inventory because support would indicate that desirability and prevalence are measuring the same thing —actual psychiatric disorder.

While Dohrenwend's second hypothesis implies a "social desirability" interpretation, his first hypothesis connotes what Nunnally (1967) terms "expressed self-desirability." Dohrenwend's first hypothesis suggests that assessments about the desirability of the items can vary independently of the prevalence of the symptoms among members of one's own group; that an individual's perceptions of what is or is not desirable can be determined by forces *external* to his traditional reference group of family, friends, or neighbors of similar socioeconomic and cultural background. This hypothesis seems to be consistent with the observation that some members of given social groups often reject characteristics common to their group. Thus, a finding that desirability and prevalence are independent (rather than redundant) predictors of mental health score suggests that a desirability bias may affect responses to Langner's inventory.

Pilot Study of Desirability and Acquiescence

An acquiescent response style, as mentioned earlier, reflects the tendency of an individual to agree (or its opposite, to disagree) to questions independently of their content. This form of acquiescence is usually thought of as a general trait which cuts across different types of personality tests and other inventories (Edwards, 1959, pp. 101–116). However, the bulk of research evidence now points to the conclusion that acquiescent response styles are of very little importance as a source of *systematic* invalidity in measuring instruments (Nunnally, 1967). Nevertheless, it is useful to examine the possible effects of an acquiescent response style on people's scores on the 22-Item Mental Health Inventory.

To test these effects and also two of Dohrenwend's hypotheses, Kevin Clancy and I conducted a pilot study to provide information for a larger scale research project with a similar objective. The hypotheses selected for testing in this study were: (1) People's scores on a psychiatric inventory are related to their assessment of the desirability of the items constituting the inventory. The more desirable the items are seen to be, the more frequently people will report (or admit to) the items. (2) People's assessment of the desirability of the inventory items reflects something other than the estimated prevalence of these symptoms among their acquaintances. Thus, desirability and estimated prevalence of symptoms are independent predictors of mental health scores. (3) People's scores on a psychiatric inventory are related to naysaying. The greater the extent of naysaying, the less the extent to which people will report (or admit to) the items.

As an initial test of these hypotheses, telephone interviews were completed with a random sample of 115 adults, representing all persons with a telephone who resided in areas of more than one million population.[1] While we recognize that some may consider telephone interviewing as inappropriate for testing hypotheses about previous studies that were based on face-to-face interviews, we feel that the comparability of the two techniques remains to be determined. Moreover, other studies (Colombotos, 1965, 1969; Meile and Haese, 1969) indicate that responses obtained by the two methods were essentially similar. Our telephone interviews (averaging seventeen minutes in length) opened with a brief introduction followed by Langner's twenty-two screening items and questions pertaining to naysaying, estimated prevalence, item desirability, and socioeconomic position. Also included were sundry marketing questions, in that the interviews were part of a nationwide marketing study.

Social Desirability of the items was measured by asking respondents to rate each of the twenty-two items on a 9-point desirability scale. Respondents were asked to look at the numbers 1

[1] The interviewing was done from a central interviewing location in New York City using local telephone lines and WATS (Wide Area Telephone Service) lines. All 115 interviews were completed in a single evening from 7:00 to 10:00 P.M. (local city time). Interviewers began in those cities in the Eastern time zone, moving across country as the hour became later. The respondents contacted represented names drawn randomly from the telephone directories of the metropolitan areas sampled. The number of completed interviews in each city was proportional to the adult population of each city relative to the combined adult population of all cities in the United States with populations of one million or greater. Hence, 23 interviews were completed in New York, representing 20 percent of the total adult population of all cities with one million or more inhabitants.

through 9 on their telephone dials. The more desirable they thought a given symptom was, the higher the number they were asked to give it. The less desirable they thought it, the lower the number they were asked to give each symptom. This procedure is somewhat similar to that developed by Edwards (1959) and employed by Dohrenwend in his study. The scores for all of the twenty-two items for each individual were summed and averaged, producing a desirability score for the twenty-two items as a whole for each respondent.

This technique was followed so as to make our findings comparable to those of Dohrenwend. We went further, however, and taking a subset of five items[2] expressing both physiological and psychological symptoms, we asked respondents: "Among your ten best friends or acquaintances, how many have each of the . . . ailments." This figure we refer to as *estimated prevalence.*

Naysaying was measured by presenting the respondents with a group of five items reflecting naysaying and five items reflecting yeasaying. The naysaying score for each individual was arrived at by substracting the number of yeasaying responses from the number of naysaying responses. In most health inventories the number of positive, "healthy" or "correct" responses (naysaying) strongly outweights the number of negative, "sickly" or "incorrect" responses (yeasaying). Hence, we expected the number of naysaying responses to exceed the number of yeasaying ones, producing a positive (+) naysaying value for each respondent.[3] The naysaying items were worded to elicit an affirmative response. They expressed health-

[2] The five items, selected at random, were: "Are you the worrying type?"; "I have personal worries that get me down physically"; "Every so often I feel hot all over"; "Do you feel somewhat apart even among friends?"; and "I am bothered by acid (sour) stomach several times a week." It would have been interesting to have also had a measure of "true prevalence" for people's friends and acquaintances as well as the measure of "estimated prevalence." Obviously, however, such a measure would be subject to the same possible limitations as those measures being considered here.

[3] Most respondents were highly discriminating in their responses to the inventory. The mean naysaying score for the total sample was 0.4, thus indicating a slight tendency toward naysaying. But it should be kept in mind that a score of 0.0 represents the presence of no response style at all. Thus, most respondents did not exhibit a strong tendency to either admit to or deny symptoms.

related symptoms which we believe are common to all Americans. Hence, the "correct" response to these items was to admit to them. Denying them was considered naysaying.[4] The yeasaying items, in contrast, were designed to elicit negative responses. They expressed health-related symptoms which we believe are physiologically impossible or, at best, improbable. Hence, the "correct" response on these items was to deny them. Admitting to them was considered yeasaying.[5]

The first step in our analysis was to calculate the mean health scores and the percentage of respondents with four or more symptoms and compare our findings with the results of the investigations of Langner, Dohrenwend, and Phillips (1966). This step was undertaken to ascertain whether the telephone interviewing techniques produced markedly different results from the personal interviewing procedure followed in other mental health studies using the twenty-two-item screening inventory. We expected that if the telephone interviews did generate different results, they would be in the direction of a higher level of mental illness. It was felt that due to the anonymity of the telephone interviewing situation, respondents might be more likely to admit to symptoms than they would be in a face-to-face interviewing situation.

Our analysis revealed that the percentage of respondents reporting four or more symptoms was fairly similar in the different studies, ranging from 27.5 percent in Phillips' New Hampshire sample up to 32.6 percent in this pilot study. Examination of the mean number of symptoms in the various studies revealed that the means too were quite similar. We tentatively conclude, therefore, that the use of a telephone interview, as opposed to a personal interview, does not markedly affect the gross results using Langner's

[4] The naysaying items and the naysaying responses (in parentheses) were: (1) "Every once in a while I feel tired" (No); (2) "I sometimes feel sleepy" (No); (3) "I have had at least one cold during the last ten years" (No); (4) "Have you ever been bothered by an upset stomach?" (Never); (5) "Have you ever felt grouchy or irritable?" (Never).

[5] The yeasaying items and the yeasaying responses (in parentheses) were: (1) "My lungs sometimes feel empty" (Yes); (2) "My teeth sometimes itch" (Yes); (3) "My heart sometimes stops beating for a few minutes" (Yes); (4) "Do you feel like the happiest person in the world?" (Always); (5) "Do your eyes ever feel cold?" (More than a few times).

mental health inventory. Hence, we believe the findings reported here may be equally applicable to the personal interview situation.

The first hypothesis tested was whether responses on the screening inventory are related to the respondent's evaluation of the desirability of the twenty-two items. Our preliminary evidence shows this to be the case (see Table 1). There are almost five times as many persons with scores of 4 or above among those who see the items as (relatively) desirable as there are among those who see them as undesirable. Comparing the mean symptom scores in the three groups reveals the same pattern.[6]

Table 1

SYMPTOM SCORES ON 22-ITEM SCREENING INSTRUMENT: BY SOCIAL DESIRABILITY OF ITEMS

	Item Desirability		
	Low (N = 39)	Medium (N = 41)	High (N = 35)
Percent With 4+ Symptoms	7.7	22.0	37.1
Mean Number of Symptoms	0.8	2.6	3.4

Chi-square = 9.40; $p < .05$
$F = 3.62$; $p < .05$

Turning now to our second hypothesis, we examine the relationship between desirability and the estimated prevalence of a subset of five symptoms within an individual's reference group.[7] Our

[6] The sample was divided into three groups of approximately equal size. The low desirability group (N = 39) had mean desirability scores of 1.6 or less. The medium desirability group (N = 41) had mean desirability scores ranging from 1.7 to 2.6, whereas the higher group (N = 35) had mean desirability scores of 2.7 or greater.

[7] Here again an attempt was made to divide the sample into three groups of approximately equal size. The distribution of the scores, however, did not allow us to meet this equal size criterion. The low prevalence group (N = 39) was characterized by mean prevalence scores of 1.5 or less. The

hypothesis is that a person's assessment concerning the desirability of the inventory items reflects something other than his estimate of the prevalence of these items in his reference group. It is clear from Table 2 that desirability and estimated prevalence are related. However, the correlation is far from perfect, and there are apparently some determinants of item desirability other than symptom prevalence among a person's friends and acquaintances. We suggested earlier that one of these other determinants is the individual's perception of the societal assessment of the desirability of the various behaviors represented by these symptoms.

Table 3 presents the independent effects of prevalence and desirability on symptom scores. The figures in Table 2 represent the mean number of symptoms reported for the five-item prevalence subscale described earlier. This table contains a number of interesting findings: (1) The two independent variables exercise a strong joint influence on mental health reporting. The mean number of symptoms among persons who report a low prevalence for their reference group and view the symptoms as undesirable is only .14, compared to a mean of 1.60 among respondents who report a medium or high reference group prevalence and view the items as relatively desirable.[8] (2) People's estimates of symptom prevalence among friends and acquaintances have an independent effect on mental health scores, at each level of desirability. (3) Item desirability too has an independent influence on mental health status within both prevalence groups. And (4) while both desirability and estimated prevalence exert independent effects on mental health ratings, the effects of desirability appear to be greater than those of prevalence.

Clearly, then, the number of symptoms that people report (or admit to) is dependent both on their perception of the prevalence of similar symptoms among friends and acquaintances and on their evaluation of the desirability of these symptoms.

---

medium prevalence group (N = 56) had mean scores ranging from 1.6 to 3.9, while the high prevalence group (N = 20) had mean scores of 4.0 or greater.

[8] It is, of course, theoretically possible that some people who do not really have a given symptom will nevertheless report it if it is something their friends have and something they see as desirable. However, we doubt that this is often the case.

Table 2

SOCIAL DESIRABILITY OF ITEMS: BY ESTIMATED PREVALENCE OF SYMPTOMS WITHIN REFERENCE GROUP

	Estimated Prevalence		
	Low (N = 39)	Medium (N = 56)	High (N = 20)
Item Desirability			
Low	53.8%	19.6%	20.0%
Medium	28.2%	34.0%	15.0%
High	17.9%	46.4%	65.0%

Chi-square = 18.43; $p < .01$

Table 3

MEAN NUMBER OF SYMPTOMS ON 5-ITEM SCREENING INSTRUMENT: BY ESTIMATED PREVALENCE OF SYMPTOMS WITHIN REFERENCE GROUP AND SOCIAL DESIRABILITY OF ITEMS

	Estimated Prevalence	
Item Desirability	Low	Medium/ High
Low	.14 (21)	.27 (15)
Medium	.27 (11)	.64 (22)
High	.86 (7)	1.60 (39)

The third hypothesis to be examined involves scores on the symptom inventory as they relate to naysaying. Table 4 shows that, as hypothesized, mental health ratings are strongly related to level of naysaying. It seems apparent from these results either that people

Table 4

SYMPTOM SCORES ON 22-ITEM SCREENING INSTRUMENT: BY NAYSAYING

	Naysaying		
	Low (N = 19)	Medium (N = 50)	High (N = 46)
Percent With 4+ Symptoms	52.6	24.0	13.0
Mean Number of Symptoms	3.6	2.2	1.7

Chi-square = 11.78; $p < .01$
F = 3.14; $p < .05$

who are naysayers are in very much better mental health than others or, as we have suggested, that they deny symptoms which they may actually experience.[9]

Table 5 contains the data necessary for examining the influence of desirability and naysaying on mental health scores. Our first observation about this table is that social desirability and naysaying are related to one another. Approximately 26 percent (18 of 69) of those who are low or medium naysayers see the items as undesirable, as compared to about 46 percent (21 of 46) of those with a high degree of naysaying. Thus, a person who is a strong naysayer is apparently more likely than others to view the symptom inventory as undesirable. A second observation is that naysaying and desirability exercise independent influences on mental health ratings—with the independent effects of desirability being larger than those of naysaying. Finally, we see quite marked joint effects of naysaying and desirability on mental health scores.

Our analysis so far suggests that Dohrenwend may be correct in raising questions about the validity of field studies of psy-

[9] We again attempted to divide the sample into groups of approximately the same size. Given the low variance in our naysaying measure, however, this task could not be accomplished. The low naysaying group (N = 19) had a mean naysaying score of −1 or less. The medium group (N = 50) had a score of 0, while the high group (N = 46) had a score of 1 or more.

Table 5

MEAN NUMBER OF SYMPTOMS ON 22-ITEM SCREENING INSTRUMENT: BY ITEM DESIRABILITY AND NAYSAYING

	Item Desirability		
Naysaying	Low	Medium	High
Low/Medium	1.1 (18)	2.6 (28)	3.6 (23)
High	0.6 (21)	2.0 (13)	2.3 (12)

chiatric disorder. We find that responses to Langner's inventory are related to both the desirability of the items and naysaying. It is not enough, however, to establish relationships between these two variables and mental health scores. Equally important is whether desirability and naysaying are themselves distributed randomly among different segments of the population. For to constitute a systematic bias, a response style must be related not only to the chief dependent variable (mental health score) but also to the independent variables of principal interest.

Since several of the "true prevalence" studies using psychiatric inventories have been concerned with the relationship between socioeconomic status and mental illness, we examine the relationships of the desirability and naysaying measures to people's position in the status hierarchy, as represented by an index combining education and income levels. Table 6 reveals that respondents' views of the desirability of the inventory items *are* significantly related to their socioeconomic status.[10] The higher their status, the less likely people are to see the items as desirable.

[10] Socioeconomic status was estimated in the following manner. All respondents from whom the information was obtained (95 of 115) were divided into four income categories (under $5000 per year, $5000–$7999, $8000–$9999, and $10,000+) and four education categories (0–8 years, 9–12, 13–15, 16+). Each respondent was given a score of 1 if his income was under $5000, a score of 2 if it was $5000–$7999, and so forth. The same procedure was followed with education. Thus the scores of 2–3 are classified as "low," those scoring 4–6 as "medium," and those 7–8 as "high."

Table 6

SOCIAL DESIRABILITY OF ITEMS: BY SOCIAL CLASS POSITION

	Social Class Position		
	Low (N = 19)	Medium (N = 46)	High (N = 30)
Mean Desirability Score	2.8	2.3	2.1
Item Desirability			
Low	26.3%	28.3%	46.7%
Medium	21.1%	43.4%	36.6%
High	52.6%	28.3%	16.7%

Chi-square = 9.62; $p < .05$

$F = 3.23$; $p < .05$

However, systematic bias has not been established if the relationship between status and desirability can be accounted for by the variable called "estimated prevalence." We have already seen (Table 2) that people's evaluation of the desirability of the symptom inventory items is strongly dependent on their estimate of the prevalence of these symptoms among their friends and acquaintances. It may be, therefore, that the reason socioeconomic position and desirability are related in Table 6 is that there is a much higher prevalence of symptoms in the lowest stratum than in the other social strata. If prevalence and desirability are related in a similar fashion in the three status groups, we might anticipate that the introduction of prevalence into the relationship between social position and desirability would tend to "interpret" the relation. Should this be the case, the association between socioeconomic status and desirability should vanish (or at least be reduced considerably) when the respondent's estimates of the prevalence of symptoms are included in the analysis.

Table 7 allows us to examine this possibility. Although the

Table 7

PERCENTAGE OF RESPONDENTS REPORTING HIGH DESIRABILITY ON 22-ITEM INDEX: BY SOCIAL CLASS POSITION AND ESTIMATED PREVALENCE WITHIN REFERENCE GROUP

	Social Class Position		
Estimated Prevalence	Low	Medium	High
Low	16.7% (6)	0.0% (13)	0.0% (8)
Medium/High	69.2% (13)	39.4% (33)	22.7% (22)

differences are masked when the medium and high prevalence groups are combined in this table, an inverse relationship between status and estimated prevalence can be seen. We also can see in Table 6 that the relation between socioeconomic status and desirability is maintained at both prevalence levels. (The relationship is stronger when there is a medium or higher prevalence of such symptoms among the people one knows than when there is a low prevalence. This means that if few of an individual's friends and acquaintances have such symptoms, he is likely to see these symptoms as undesirable—whatever his location in the status hierarchy. But if such complaints are rather common among a man's acquaintances, then his socioeconomic position makes a larger difference in evaluating the desirability of the symptoms items.)

Our main concern, however, is about whether the relationship between status and desirability could be accounted for by the respondents' estimated prevalence of symptoms among people they know. Clearly, this is not the case. Tables 5 and 6 show that people's views of the desirability of the inventory items *are* independently related to their socioeconomic position. Hence, we conclude that desirability, at least in our sample, does constitute a source of bias and possible invalidity.

Before examining the implications of response bias involving desirability, let us consider the relationship between the second source of possible invalidity in our investigation—naysaying and class position. Examination of these data reveals that the association between the two variables does not reach statistical significance.[11] Thus, we must tentatively conclude with regard to naysaying that although our earlier data support Dohrenwend's hypothesis that an acquiescent response style is related to scores on the twenty-two-item inventory, we find no evidence that naysaying is distributed in the different social strata in a nonrandom fashion. Our data do not, therefore, support Dohrenwend's contention that field studies of psychiatric disorder among different social strata may have validity problems due to a response set traceable to acquiescence.

We see, then, that of two possible sources of invalidity, only desirability exercises a systematic influence on people's responses to the items in Langner's mental health inventory. But the implications of even this one source of bias are considerable. For it appears likely that the frequently demonstrated inverse relationship between social class and mental illness may be due partially to the fact that people's perceptions of the desirability of the items constituting some measures of mental health status are related both to their social class position and to their willingness to admit to certain symptoms of mental illness. Thus, the higher prevalence of mental disorder in the lower classes may be explained by the finding that lower-class persons regard the behaviors in question as less undesirable than do persons of higher class standing and are, therefore, more likely to report (or admit to) these experiences, feelings, and behaviors.

Let us look at the empirical evidence for this assertion. We consider the biasing effects of symptom desirability first by looking at the relationship between socioeconomic position and mental health and then by examining the same relation with the introduction of a desirability measure. We find a mean of 3.4 symptoms in the lower strata, compared to means of 2.1 and 1.6 at the other status levels—a difference between the two extremes of 1.8 in the mean number of psychiatric symptoms. After adding the desirability measure in Table 8 we find that among those who view the items as very undesirable the difference in the mean number of symptoms between low and high SES persons is only 0.8. Among people who

[11] Table supplied on request.

Table 8

MEAN NUMBER OF SYMPTOMS ON 22-ITEM SCREENING INSTRUMENT: BY SOCIAL CLASS POSITION AND DESIRABILITY OF ITEMS

	Social Class Position		
Item Desirability	Low	Medium	High
Low	1.6 (5)	0.5 (13)	0.8 (14)
Medium/High	4.0 (14)	2.8 (33)	2.3 (16)

see the items as less undesirable, the SES difference is 1.7, or about the same as between the top and bottom symptom scores. In other words, this analysis reveals that the relationship between socioeconomic position and mental health *is* affected by people's evaluations of the desirability of the mental health inventory items. But these results also confirm that the existence of a relationship between socioeconomic status and mental disorder is *not* just an artifact of the hypothesized distortions arising from response bias.[12]

Conclusions and Implications

There are two ways of regarding this pilot study's results concerning the biasing effects of response styles as they affect the

[12] It is important to note in Table 7 that the desirability of the twenty-two mental health items has a greater influence on people's scores on the mental health index than does their social class position. In order to consider the relationship in "proportional reduction in error" terms (Costner, 1965), the data were subjected to a linear regression analysis. Mental health scores were predicted on the twenty-two-item inventory using the mean desirability score for the twenty-two items and the social class measures. The multiple R for these two variables in predicting scores on the mental health index was .49 ($p < .01$). Thus, almost one-fourth of the variance in the dependent variable is accounted for by social class and desirability. Of this, about 56 percent of the variance *accounted for* can be attributed to the desirability of the items, with the partial r for desirability being .37 ($p < .01$). The remainder of the variance accounted for can be traced to our measure of socioeconomic status, which is a partial r of —.32 ($p < .01$).

relationship between socioeconomic status and mental illness. On the one hand, these results might be seen as lending further support to the stability and strength of the relation between SES and disorder. For, it might be argued, if acquiescence does not constitute a systematic bias in the relation between socioeconomic position and mental health measures, and if social desirability (which does exercise a systematic bias) only partially accounts for the relationship between the two variables, then the results increase our confidence in the validity of findings with regard to the relationship between social class and mental illness. On the other hand, these results may be viewed as casting some doubt on field studies of mental illness. For while acquiescence did not constitute a response bias, the influence of the social desirability bias was considerable. As was noted, more of the total variance in mental health scores was accounted for by social desirability than by socioeconomic status.

In that this one biasing factor does have considerable influence on people's mental health scores, I believe the simultaneous examination of other variables found to exercise biasing effects in social research would reveal the existence of sizable bias and invalidity in studies of mental illness. Although subject to conflicting interpretations, studies by Rosenberg (1965b) on "evaluation apprehension," Crowne and Marlowe (1964) on "social approval," Rosenthal (1966) on "modeling" and "expectancy" effects all point to a variety of factors which may lower the validity of social science measuring instruments. The study by Clark and Tifft (1966) also raises important questions about the validity of certain sociological measures.

With such a high percentage of sociological research involving the use of field interviews and questionnaires to study various social phenomena, it is somewhat surprising that there have been so few studies concerned with the possible biasing effects of contaminating methodological artifacts. Even studies of so-called deviant behavior have given little empirical attention to problems of response bias. This is true despite the warning of such writers as Maccoby and Maccoby (1954, p. 482) who caution that "when people are being interviewed (or are filling out questionnaires) directly concerning behavior about which there is a strong expectation of social approval or disapproval, and in which there is considerable ego-involvement, they tend to err in the direction of idealizing their behavior."

The findings of the pilot study reported here, when considered together with the recent investigations of Dohrenwend (1966) and of Phillips and Segal (1969), do seem to raise some important questions about at least one type of deviant behavior—mental illness—as it is examined in relation to other social phenomena in field settings using interviews. These findings also suggest the possibility of similar biases in other studies involving social class. Consider, for instance, studies of happiness and of racial prejudice. Such investigations have consistently revealed greater happiness and less racial prejudice among middle-class persons than among people from lower social strata. While the results of such studies may, indeed, represent "true" differences among the various social classes, an alternative possibility is that middle-class individuals are more aware than lower-class persons are as to what are considered the most socially desirable responses to questions concerning happiness and racial prejudice. Thus they may be unwilling to give what are, for middle-class individuals, "undesirable" responses. I do not know which is the case, but I hope that other investigators will consider more seriously the need for paying greater attention to the validation of social science measuring instruments. While validation is clearly a difficult problem, it is also clear that measurement issues, as Blalock (1969) has observed, constitute the key to the advancement of any science.

★★★★★★★★★★★★★★★★

3

Social Desirability and Invalidity

★★★★★★★★★★★★★★★★

Since sociology is variously defined as the study (or "science") of "interaction," "human relationships," "human behavior," or "social processes," one might expect that the principal modes of data collection would involve the actual observation of behavior and interaction. As we all know, this is not the case. For sociological researchers to a large extent rely on those people who are the objects of their investigations to *report* their own behavior. As Coleman (1969, p. 109) notes: "most research techniques which analyze behavioral data take a short cut in data collection, and base their methods on individuals' reports of their own behavior and, less frequently, on those of others." And Webb and his associates (1966) point out that the dominant mass of social science today, especially in sociology, is based on people's reports in questionnaires and interviews.[1]

[1] A rough idea of just how dominant these two data collection pro-

While sociologists have become increasingly sophisticated with regard to data-analysis procedures, they have not devoted equal attention to problems of data collection and measurement. And Hauser (1969), among others, asserts that the problem of adequate measurement is *the* major block to progress in sociological research. One way to consider these problems is to note that whenever sociologists collect data from people, differences among individuals on various measures arise both from "true" differences in the characteristic (attribute, quality, or whatever) which one is attempting to measure and from errors in the measurement process. So the investigator has the major task of determining which differences are real and which are variations due to measurement errors.

The sociological investigator would like measures of both his independent and dependent variables to be valid and reliable. Furthermore, he generally tries to minimize, eliminate, or control for various extraneous factors that may affect the relationship between his independent and dependent variables: he wants to assure that his findings are valid. Some independent variables of interest to sociologists undoubtedly have measurement problems, such as those involved in the relationship between authoritarianism or alienation and voting. But more often, the independent variable is rather solidly established—age, sexual status, education, and marital status are examples of variables which can be measured with relative validity and reliability.

Measures of dependent variables, on the other hand, are frequently much more problematic in nature and much more subject to inaccuracy. In some instances, the accuracy of interview and questionnaire data can be checked against some outside criteria (such as voting and other records). Although this checking has not often been done, it has been done enough to reveal considerable discrepancies between people's verbal reports and the outside criteria, as I mentioned in Chapter One. It is obviously very difficult to find ways of validating people's responses and reports with regard to

---

cedures are in sociology can be derived from the results of Brown and Gilmartin's examination (1969) of research articles published in the *American Sociological Review* and the *American Journal of Sociology* during 1965–1966. They found that more than 90 percent of the research articles based on primary data had utilized interviews or questionnaires or both.

such things as mental health status, religiosity, marital happiness, work satisfaction, alienation, prejudice, values, and a whole host of other subjects of interest to sociological investigators.

Probably because these validation procedures are so hard to locate many sociologists seem content to ignore problems regarding the validity of both their measurements and their results. The common failure to tackle these problems is also partially responsible for the fact that there are almost as many different measures as there are studies of social phenomena. For example, Bonjean and others (1967, pp. 9–10) found in their examination of all articles and research notes in four major sociological journals over a twelve-year period that "there were 3,609 attempts to measure various phenomena by the use of scales and indices and 2,080 different measures were used. Of the measures used, only 589 (28.3 percent of the total numbers of scales and indices) were used more than once . . . 2.26 percent were used more than five times." Because validity issues are so often overlooked, one measure appears to be regarded as being as good as another.

Among the hundreds of empirical studies published annually by sociologists only a tiny fraction pay serious attention to bias and invalidity. For example, a survey of family research instruments by Strauss (1964, p. 368) revealed that "all but a few of the 263 instruments surveyed were conceived without benefit of validating procedures." In an attempt to deal with bias and invalidity in survey studies, Kevin Clancy and I undertook a series of investigations to examine these problems.[2] Our research differs from that of most previous investigations of bias, which usually have attempted to take stock of respondent bias in a post hoc manner so as to "make sense" out of sometimes discrepant or unexpected findings. Although biases may arise from a variety of sources, our specific concern was with respondent bias resulting from considerations of social desirability. In the study presented in the previous chapter, we found that social desirability was related to both class position and to mental health scores and thus constituted a systematic bias in the relationship between social class position and mental health status.

These results led us to examine the effects of two different

[2] This research was partially supported by Grant 1 R03 MH18900-01, National Institute of Mental Health.

components of social desirability on several measures of interest to sociological investigators. As noted in the previous chapter, social desirability as a response determinant refers to the tendency of people to deny socially undesirable traits or qualities and to admit to socially desirable ones. However, the response is seen in two different ways in the literature: sometimes as a personality construct, sometimes as a quality of the measurement items. The former is termed *need for social approval;* the latter, *trait desirability.*

Considering need for approval first, Crowne and Marlowe (1964, p. 354) define it as "the need of subjects to respond in culturally sanctioned ways." They argue that people who score high on their scale of social approval are those who (p. 27) "conform to social stereotypes of what is good to acknowledge concerning oneself in order to achieve approval from others." A number of their studies found support for this thesis. For example, subjects who scored high in need for social approval gave favorable attitude ratings to an extremely boring experimental task, gave popular word associations, set cautious goals in a risk-taking situation, and were more susceptible to persuasion. But as Robinson and Shaver (1969, p. 638) point out, "this research . . . has been conducted with college students and therefore leaves unanswered the importance of such response sets among less-educated persons in sample surveys."

Turning now to trait desirability, Edwards (1953, 1957, 1959) and, more recently, Dohrenwend (1966) focus on people's tendency to endorse statements on the basis of their implicit social desirability rather than on their actual explicit content. For example, the possible effects of social desirability can be seen in the suggestion by Cook and Selltiz (1964, p. 39) that people will attempt to give responses that will place them in a favorable light: "well adjusted, unprejudiced, rational, open minded, and democratic." Edwards (1953) was apparently the first to find empirical evidence for the simple observation that there is a relationship between the judged desirability of a response in a self-report study and the likelihood of an individual's giving that response. And his findings have been replicated in numerous psychological investigations (Cowen and Tongas, 1959; Rosen, 1956; and Wiggins and Rumrill, 1959). For the most part, however, these investigations have focused on the influence of people's judgments of social desirability on their responses to various personality measures and have generally restricted their inquiries to samples of college students.

The study of social desirability in survey studies is important for at least three reasons. First, since many sociological measures involve drawing inferences from self-reports of beliefs, feelings, behaviors, and so on, we should expect a great deal of distortion in overt responses. As Cook and Selltiz (1964, p. 331) have pointed out regarding self-report measures: "The purpose of the instrument is obvious to the respondent; the implications of his answers are apparent to him; he can consciously control his responses. Thus a person who wishes to give a certain picture of himself—whether in order to impress the tester favorably, to preserve his own self-image, or for some other reason—can rather easily do so." Though this problem of social desirability has long been recognized and dealt with explicitly by psychologists, sociologists have paid less attention to its possible effects in survey studies. Such techniques as assuring anonymity, emphasizing the importance of "honest" answers, creating rapport, and stressing that there are "no right or wrong answers" are designed to make it easier for respondents to give answers that may be considered socially undesirable, but despite such precautions, respondents may still be affected by considerations of social desirability. This study examines that possibility.

Second, if it is true that considerations of social desirability affect people's responses, then the validity of sociological measures may be called into question; and third, the existence of social desirability influences may affect the validity of the investigator's results. These reasons underscore the relevance of Herbert Hyman's remarks (1954, p. 4) concerning the importance of detecting errors in social science investigations: "All scientific inquiry is subject to error, and it is far better to be aware of this, to study the sources in an attempt to reduce it, and to estimate the magnitude of such errors in our findings, than to be ignorant of the errors concealed in the data. One must not equate ignorance of error with the lack of error. The lack of demonstration of error in certain fields of inquiry often derives from the existence of methodological research into the problem and merely denotes a less advanced stage of that profession."

A fourth reason for studying the effects of possible errors, biases, artifacts, and response determinants in survey studies is that such variables as social desirability may come to be seen as interesting and important sociological phenomena in their own right, rather than as contaminants to be eliminated from sociological investigations (McGuire, 1969).

Hypotheses

We believe that people's responses in many sociological investigations are affected by both their judgments of the trait desirability of interview and questionnaire items and by their need for social approval. Thus, we tested these possibilities by examining the effects of people's judgments of trait desirability and their need for approval on their responses to questions pertaining to a number of areas of interest to sociological investigators: overall happiness, religiosity, number of friends, marital happiness, prejudice, and visiting a doctor. We advanced the following hypotheses for testing: (1) The more desirable people's assessment of the traits, the greater the extent to which they will report: being very happy, being very religious, having many friends, being very happily married, being nonprejudiced, and visiting a doctor. (2) The greater people's need for social approval, the greater the extent to which they will report these six characteristics.

Methods

In order to test these hypotheses, telephone interviews were completed with a random sample of 404 adults representing all households with a listed telephone who resided in the New England and Mid-Atlantic states. *General happiness* was measured by a single three-alternative question used by previous investigators (Bradburn, 1969; Bradburn and Caplovitz, 1965; Gurin, Veroff, and Feld, 1958; Phillips, 1967): "Taking all things together, how would you say things are these days—would you say you're very happy, pretty happy, or not too happy these days?" *Religiosity* was measured by the question: "How religious would you say you are—very religious, somewhat religious, or not at all religious?" *Number of friends* was estimated by asking: "Thinking of people, including relatives, whom you consider really good friends—that is, people you feel free to talk with about personal things—about how many such friends would you say you have?" *Marital happiness* was measured by responses to questions by previous researchers (Orden and Bradburn, 1968, 1969): "Taking all things together, how would you describe your marriage? Would you say that your marriage was very happy, pretty happy, or not too happy?" *Prejudice* was estimated by asking: "If you went to a party and found that most of the people were of a racial or ethnic group different from your own, would you be very bothered, somewhat bothered, or not bothered at all?" *Doctor visits* were determined by asking people to respond "yes" or "no" to the statement "I visit my doctor at least once a year."

Trait desirability was measured by having respondents rate each of the above items on a nine-point scale of desirability. The more desirable they thought a characteristic to be, the higher the number they were asked to give it. The less desirable they thought it, the lower the number they were asked to give it.[3] This procedure is similar to that developed by Edwards (1959) and employed by Dohrenwend (1966) and in the pilot study described in Chapter Two.

Need for social approval was measured by using a shortened version of the Crowne and Marlowe (1964) instrument.[4] This scale includes such items as "I never hesitate to go out of my way to help someone in trouble" and "There have been times when I feel like rebelling against people in authority."

Findings

The first hypothesis tested was whether responses to the various questions are related to the respondents' evaluations of the

[3] The items were sometimes worded in a positive direction (that is, "To be the kind of person who is happily married") and sometimes in a negative one (such as, "To have few friends"). In our tabular presentations, however, we have taken these differences into account in classifying people as high, medium, and low with regard to desirability.

[4] The Crowne-Marlowe scale was administered to a sample of thirty-two adult respondents in January 1969, and the resulting data were subjected to an item analysis. Using a step-wise multiple regression program, ten items were identified which produced a .84 correlation (Pearson-multiple r) with the total score. These items constitute the instruments used in this research.

desirability of the various characteristics being measured. The results presented in Table 9 show that this relationship exists. Although the differences are of unequal magnitude, there is a consistent pattern showing that people who see a characteristic as highly desirable[5] report themselves as higher on that characteristic (happiness, religiosity, and so on) than do people who see the trait as undesirable. Thus, our first hypothesis is supported.

These findings are consistent with those reported in the previous chapter, where we found that people's scores on a psychiatric inventory were strongly related to their assessments of the desirability of the items constituting the inventory. Although that investigation and the present study both reason that whether or not people *report* or *admit* certain factors or characteristics about themselves is dependent on their assessments of the social desirability of such characteristics, there is another possible line of reasoning regarding these relationships—people who find certain things desirable choose to have views and actions consistent with their evaluations of desirability. Thus, it might be argued that "of course" people who see visiting a doctor as desirable will be more likely to visit a doctor than those who see it as undesirable. From that point of view they act *because* it is desirable that they do so. Similarly, with being religious, nonprejudiced, and having many friends: if people place a high value on such characteristics they will act accordingly. While such a line of reasoning is plausible, it fails to explain why people's mental health status or marital and general happiness should be related to their assessments of trait desirability. For it seems difficult to argue that *because* people see marital happiness as highly desirable, for instance, they are able to choose to be very happily married.

We have, then, two alternate explanations for the causes of people's assessments of the desirability of various characteristics. Our own view is that some people *distort* (either purposefully or for other reasons) their responses to survey questions because they see some characteristics as being desirable or undesirable. The other line of argument is that people's responses are accurate (not distorted) and that the association between their responses and their

[5] For each of the social desirability traits, an attempt was made to divide the sample into groups of approximately equal size.

Table 9

RESPONSES ON SIX MEASURES BY SOCIAL DESIRABILITY OF TRAITS

	Trait Desirability		
	High	Medium	Low
(1) % very happy	36.5	29.6	15.6
	(249)[a]	(108)	(45)
(2) % very religious	38.2	22.5	6.2
	(149)	(102)	(145)
(3) % seven or more friends	39.1	31.5	31.2
	(166)	(111)	(112)
(4) % very happily married	78.6	72.2	25.0
	(248)	(36)	(16)
(5) % nonprejudiced[b]	82.5	62.2	63.3
	(252)	(82)	(60)
(6) % visited a doctor	83.4	79.4	44.3
	(229)	(97)	(77)
(7) % high in overclaiming	28.2	23.2	11.0
	(124)	(162)	(118)

[a]This represents the actual number of people who saw the happiness trait as highly desirable. These numbers are included since the case base differs for the social desirability items.

[b]These are the people who answered they would "not be bothered at all" to the prejudice question.

assessments of trait desirability reflects the true state of affairs, in the world outside the interview situation. One way of choosing between these two possibilities might be as follows. Imagine that we are interested in the relationship between people's assessments as to the desirability of being someone who voted in all elections and their reports of having voted in a specific election. If we had access to the voting records (and if they were accurate), we could then choose between the two explanations on the basis of the degree of discrepancy between people's verbal responses and the records. Support for our view would come from a finding that people's actual voting behavior was *unrelated* both to their verbal responses and to their assessments of the desirability of being someone who was a voter.

The alternative explanation would gain support from a finding that people's actual voting behavior was strongly *related* to both verbal responses and assessments of trait desirability. Clearly, however, this procedure would be difficult and expensive to employ.

Therefore, we attempted to gather data that would provide another way to choose between the two explanations. Following the procedure used with the items in Table 8, we obtained assessments of the desirability of: being the kind of person who tries new products, reads all of the latest books, knows something about the latest television programs, and has seen all of the newest movies.[6] We also asked them questions regarding their use of several new products, books, television programs, and movies—all of which were actually nonexistent. Those high on this "dissimulation" index we term *overclaimers*. Item (7) in Table 9 shows the relationship between people's responses and their assessments of these characteristics. Those who saw the traits as highly desirable are more than twice as likely to give what we know to be "inaccurate" responses than are those who saw the characteristics as highly undesirable. Because of this evidence, we feel that our initial line of reasoning is preferable to the alternative explanation offered above.[7]

Considering now our second hypothesis, we examine the relationship between respondents' need for social approval and their responses to the various questions. Our expectation is that people who are high in the need for social approval will be "higher" on the various items than will those with a lower need for social approval. Table 10 shows that this hypothesis is supported, albeit somewhat weakly, by our findings; there is a consistent pattern in the hypothesized direction but the differences between those high and low in the need for social approval are generally quite small. Still, the con-

[6] Respondents were asked to rate desirability on a nine-point scale, as with the other measures employed in this investigation.

[7] A third possibility is that people who have a trait (or characteristic, or whatever) therefore find it desirable. For example, people who report having seen nonexistent movies may, as a consequence, say they find it very desirable to be the kind of person who sees the latest movies. Even if the causal sequence runs in that direction, it is still the case that their response with regard to having seen a nonexistent movie (or reading a book, and so on) is *inaccurate*. A fourth possibility is that people's judgments as to the desirability of various traits are inaccurate, while their responses are accurate. This last possibility seems highly unlikely.

Table 10

RESPONSES ON SIX MEASURES BY NEED FOR SOCIAL APPROVAL

	Need for Social Approval		
	High	Medium	Low
(1) % very happy	41.7	33.5	25.2
	(102)[a]	(155)	(143)
(2) % very religious	24.0	25.2	18.0
	(100)	(155)	(140)
(3) % seven or more friends	41.8	35.3	29.1
	(98)	(150)	(141)
(4) % very happily married	81.9	74.6	63.2
	(72)	(122)	(117)
(5) % nonprejudiced[b]	77.0	80.5	68.6
	(100)	(154)	(140)
(6) % visited a doctor	76.7	78.8	69.4
	(103)	(156)	(144)
(7) % high in overclaiming	21.4	26.9	13.8
	(103)	(156)	(145)

[a] This represents the actual number of people who are high in the need for social approval. These numbers are included since the case base for various levels of social approval differs.

[b] These are the people who answered they would "not be bothered at all" to the prejudice question.

sistency of the patterns does show that need for social approval affects people's responses.

Let us now examine the interactive effects of need for social approval and assessments of trait desirability on people's responses to the various questions. Contrary to what might be expected, evaluations of trait desirability are generally unrelated to people's need for social approval.[8] Thus, whether or not people see various traits as socially desirable is not determined by the personality characteristic of need for social approval. This is an interesting finding and

[8] The only exceptions to this were slight tendencies for those high in the need for social approval to see marital happiness and religiosity as more desirable than did those lower in the need for social approval.

one that, as far as we know, has not been reported by previous investigators—who have focused on either trait desirability or social approval, but not on the relationship between them.

Table 11 shows the joint effects of need for social approval and trait desirability on people's responses to a specific question. It indicates that need for social approval and assessments of trait desirability exercise strong *joint* effects on people's responses. Considering general happiness, for example, we find that 49.4 percent of those respondents who both have a high need for social approval and see happiness as highly desirable report themselves as being "very happy"; whereas only 8.3 percent of those with a low need for approval who see happiness as relatively undesirable report being "very happy."

The same general relationships are found for the other six measures. Contrary to what might be expected, there are no clear patterns with regard to interactive effects. While we would have anticipated that the effects of trait desirability would have been most pronounced among those with a high need for social approval, this clearly is not the case. Furthermore, Table 11 indicates that, with the exception of "religiosity" and "doctor visits" among those seeing such visits as low in desirability, social approval continues to exercise an independent effect on people's responses. And, without exception, judgments of trait desirability exercise an independent influence on responses throughout. As would be expected from the findings in the previous tables, trait desirability generally has a greater influence than need for approval on people's responses.

What we have shown thus far, then, is that two possible response determinants—trait desirability and need for social approval—which are generally unrelated to one another are independently related to people's responses concerning various sociological measures. In that trait desirability generally exercises a stronger influence than does need for social approval on peoples' responses, we now turn to a demonstration of how this factor influences the relationships between the various measures (religiosity, and so on) and one of the most "solidly" established independent variables employed by sociological investigators: sexual status.

Table 12 shows the "original" relationships between sexual status and the various measures before introducing trait desirability

Table 11

RESPONSES ON SIX MEASURES: BY NEED FOR SOCIAL APPROVAL AND SOCIAL DESIRABILITY OF TRAITS

	NEED FOR SOCIAL APPROVAL								
	High			*Medium*			*Low*		
	High Desir.	Medium Desir.	Low Desir.	High Desir.	Medium Desir.	Low Desir.	High Desir.	Medium Desir.	Low Desir.
(1) % very happy	49.4 (62)[a]	28.0 (31)	33.3 (9)	38.0 (92)	35.0 (40)	12.5 (24)	27.3 (95)	24.3 (37)	8.3 (12)
(2) % very religious	34.9 (43)	23.1 (26)	9.7 (31)	42.2 (64)	23.7 (38)	5.7 (53)	35.7 (42)	21.1 (38)	3.3 (60)
(3) % seven or more friends	47.7 (44)	34.6 (26)	39.3 (28)	30.4 (56)	40.8 (49)	15.6 (39)	40.9 (66)	22.2 (36)	15.4 (39)
(4) % very happily married	82.5 (63)		77.8[b] (9)	81.7 (93)		48.4[b] (31)	72.8 (92)		28.0[b] (25)
(5) % nonprejudiced[c]	82.8 (64)	69.6 (23)	61.5 (13)	87.1 (101)	63.0 (27)	73.1 (26)	77.0 (87)	56.3 (32)	52.4 (21)
(6) % visited a doctor	82.5 (57)	92.3 (26)	40.0 (20)	90.1 (91)	79.4 (34)	45.2 (31)	76.6 (81)	70.1 (37)	46.1 (26)
(7) % high in over-claiming	28.2 (39)	22.6 (31)	12.1 (33)	33.3 (51)	28.8 (66)	15.4 (39)	20.6 (34)	15.4 (65)	6.5 (46)

[a] This represents the actual number of people who are both high in the need for social approval and see the item (trait) as highly desirable. The numbers are included since the case base differs for various combinations of need for approval and trait desirability.

[b] Here, medium and low trait desirability are combined because of the small number of cases.

[c] These are the people who answered that they would "not be bothered at all" to the prejudice question.

into the analysis. For five of the seven measures in the table, women are "higher" than men. In most cases, the relationships between sex and the various measures are rather modest in magnitude. We next turn to an examination of the relationship between our chief independent variable (sexual status) and the "test factor"—in this case, people's judgments of the desirability of each of the seven traits. Inspection of Table 13 reveals no consistent pattern with regard to these relationships. With some traits (marital happiness and nonprejudice) there is virtually no relationship to sex; with two traits (overall happiness and number of friends) men give higher assessments of desirability; and with three others (religiosity, doctor visits, and being up on things) women give higher desirability ratings. Given the generally small magnitude of these associations, it is unlikely that any relationships found between sexual status and people's responses will be "interpreted" by the influence of trait desirability. Nevertheless, trait desirability may effect the relationships in other ways. Let us examine this possibility.

Table 12

SEXUAL STATUS AND RESPONSES TO VARIOUS MEASURES

	Sexual Status		
	Males	Females	Yule's Q
(1) % very happy	28.5 (200)	36.1 (202)	.18
(2) % very religious	18.0 (200)	27.0 (196)	.26
(3) % very happily married	70.1 (150)	73.1 (156)	.07
(4) % visiting a doctor	70.0 (200)	80.0 (204)	.26
(5) % high overclaiming	18.5 (200)	23.0 (204)	.15
(6) % seven or more friends	41.4 (193)	27.7 (202)	—.28
(7) % nonprejudiced	78.8 (197)	72.4 (197)	—.19

Table 13

SEXUAL STATUS AND SOCIAL DESIRABILITY OF TRAITS

	Sexual Status		
	Males (N = 200)	Females (N = 204)	Yule's Q
Percent Seeing Traits as Highly Desirable			
Being very happy	65.0	58.3	—.15
Being very religious	32.0	43.4	.23
Being maritally very happy	75.8	76.3	.00
Visiting the doctor	52.5	61.3	.16
Being "up" on things	24.0	37.2	.30
Having many friends	46.6	38.6	—.16
Being nonprejudiced	65.0	63.0	—.04

For ease of presentation and discussion, we will show the effects of trait desirability on the relationships between sex and the various measures in Table 14, referring the reader back to Table 12 for comparisons with the original relationships. To begin with, we found in Table 12 that sex and happiness were related, with a somewhat higher percentage of women than men reporting that they were "very happy." However, an interesting finding emerges when trait desirability is introduced into the analysis in Table 14. Among those who see happiness as highly desirable, the magnitude of the original relationship (Q = .18) is increased considerably (Q = .32). But among those seeing happiness as less desirable[9] the relationship is now reversed (Q = —.03). Thus, the relationship between our independent variable (sexual status) and an overall measurement of happiness is *specified* through the introduction of

[9] The "less" category includes those with both medium and low scores with regard to trait desirability.

trait desirability; only among those viewing happiness as highly desirable do women report a higher level of happiness than do men. Among "low" desirability respondents there is virtually no relationship between sex and report of happiness. Two other observations need to be made regarding the effects of trait desirability on happiness. The influence of desirability on people's responses is more pronounced among women than among men, and trait desirability exercises a stronger influence than sexual status on people's reports of happiness.

Consider now the influence of trait desirability on the other relationships. We saw in Table 12 that a higher percentage of women than men were "very religious," "very happily married," visited the doctor at least once a year, and were what we call overclaimers. When trait desirability is introduced into each of these four relationships, we see the following: (1) the strength of the original relationship between sex and religiosity ($Q = .26$) is increased among those seeing religiosity as very desirable ($Q = .31$) and virtually disappears ($Q = .04$) among other respondents; (2) the original weak relationship between sex and reports of marital happiness ($Q = .07$) is stronger among those seeing marital happiness as highly desirable ($Q = .24$) and also in the opposite direction ($Q = -.39$) among those seeing it as less desirable; (3) the relationship between sexual status and doctor visits is virtually unaffected by judgments of trait desirability; and (4) the original relationship between sex and overclaiming ($Q = .15$) is increased among those seeing the trait as very desirable ($Q = .22$) and vanishes among other respondents.

Looking at the other two measures in the table, when trait desirability is introduced into the relationship between sexual status and friends, once again the original relationship ($Q = .28$) is stronger among those seeing the trait as something highly desirable ($Q = -.44$) than among those viewing it as less desirable. For the prejudice measure, however, the relationship is again specified by the introduction of trait desirability—but this time the relationship is stronger among those who do not see the trait as highly desirable.

To review, with six of the seven measures (all but doctor visits), the magnitude of the original relationship between sexual status and people's responses is specified by the introduction of

Table 14

SEXUAL STATUS AND RESPONSES TO VARIOUS MEASURES: BY TRAIT DESIRABILITY

	Sexual Status		
	Males	Females	Yule's Q
	(1) (% Very happy)		
Trait Desirability			
High	29.8 (130)	43.7 (119)	.32
Low	26.1 (70)	25.3 (83)	—.03
	Q = .10	Q = .40	
	(2) (% Very religious)		
Trait Desirability			
High	29.7 (64)	44.7 (85)	.31
Low	12.5 (136)	13.5 (111)	.04
	Q = .48	Q = .67	
	(3) (% Very happily married)		
Trait Desirability			
High	78.7 (119)	85.7 (119)	.24
Low	62.9 (27)	42.9 (28)	—.39
	Q = .38	Q = .78	
	(4) (% Visiting a doctor)		
Trait Desirability			
High	80.0 (105)	86.4 (124)	.21
Low	58.9 (95)	69.6 (79)	.24
	Q = .47	Q = .45	
	(5) (% High overclaimers)		
Trait Desirability			
High	22.9 (48)	31.6 (76)	.22
Low	17.6 (152)	18.0 (128)	.00
	Q = .18	Q = .36	

Table 14

SEXUAL STATUS AND RESPONSES TO VARIOUS MEASURES: BY TRAIT DESIRABILITY (cont.)

	Sexual Status		
	Males	Females	Yule's Q
	(6) (% Seven or more friends)		
Trait Desirability			
High	48.9 (90)	27.6 (76)	−.44
Low	34.9 (103)	28.2 (126)	−.16
	Q = .28	Q = .00	
	(7) (% Nonprejudiced)		
Trait Desirability			
Low	82.0 (128)	83.1 (124)	.03
High	72.6 (69)	61.8 (63)	−.25
	Q = .26	Q = .30	

judgments of trait desirability into the analysis. And with four of the measures, both the magnitude and direction of the relationships are specified. Clearly, then, people's assessments of the desirability of the items do affect the relationship between their sexual status and their responses to such items.

The above results, however, are not the only points of interest in Table 14. First, the independent effects of trait desirability on people's responses are generally greater among women than among men. For instance, the relationship between judgments of trait desirability and report of happiness is .40 among women and only .10 among men. Similarly, for measures of religiosity, marital happiness, prejudice, and overclaiming, the relationships are stronger among women. With one item (number of friends) the relationship is stronger among men, and with one (doctor visits) there is virtually no difference between the sexes. This tendency for women to be more affected than men by considerations of the relative desirability of various traits may indicate a greater sensitivity among women than men to providing the "right" answers. Women's generally greater susceptibility to the influence of societal norms and values may be evidenced in the interview situation as well as in the larger society (see McGuire, 1968).

Second, the independent effects of trait desirability on people's responses are consistently stronger than the independent effects of sex. On all but one measure (number of friends), people's responses are more strongly influenced by their assessments of the desirability of the characteristics being asked about than by their sexual status. This finding is similar to what we found in our pilot study (Chapter Two), where more of the total variance in people's mental health scores was accounted for by social desirability than by socioeconomic position.

Thus, three general patterns have emerged from the introduction of people's assessments of trait desirability into the relationship between their sexual status and their responses to a number of questions regarding various social phenomena. To begin with, the relationships between sex and responses were influenced by trait desirability. In some instances, the magnitude of the relationships was affected; in others, the direction of the relationships. In addition, the effects of social desirability were consistently stronger among women than among men. And finally, the effects of judgments of trait desirability on people's responses were consistently greater than the effects of sexual status.

Discussion

If, as most sociologists assume, people's behavior is partially a product of their needs, values, and expectations, it is not surprising that their behavior (responses) in interview situations will also be affected by these factors. The theoretical writings of Cicourel (1964) and Riecken (1962) and the substantive results of inquiries by Rosenthal (1966), Friedman (1967) and several other social psychologists all indicate that in social science investigations—as in many other social activities—people tend to organize their behavior in light of what they feel the "others" (interviewer, observer, laboratory experimenter) will expect is appropriate for someone like them in that kind of situation. Thus, Riecken speaks of the subject's desire to "put his best foot forward." And Rosenberg (1965b, 1969) speaks of "evaluation apprehension" which he defines as "an active anxiety-toned concern that he (the subject) win a positive evaluation from the experimenter, or at least that he provide no grounds for a negative one." Psychologists have been generally unsuccessful in eliminating the influence of such tendencies on the dependent variables of interest, as have we in the present research. For despite the fact that we follow the usual precautions (assuring anonymity, stressing that there are no right or wrong answers, and so on) for eliminating the possible effects of desirability factors, our respondents were, as we have seen, very much affected by considerations of social desirability. It might be, of course, that had we not followed these precautionary procedures, the relationships between the two measures of social desirability (trait desirability and need for approval) and people's responses on the various items would have been even stronger. Whether or not this could happen, our data indicate quite clearly that taking the usual "precautions" will not eliminate the influence of people's desire to place themselves in a favorable light on many measures of interest to sociological investigators.

The results presented here raise serious questions about the validity of sociological measuring instruments. Even though the measures of happiness, religiosity, and so on included in this study were single-item measures, there is reason to believe that multiple-item measures are also influenced by social desirability factors, as was shown in Chapter Two. We must conclude, then, that measures of happiness, religiosity, and the other measures included here are not measuring what they are purported to measure; their validity is called into question (Cannell and Kahn, 1968). As Selltiz and others (1963, p. 277) have noted, "many—probably most—questionnaires and interviews have been used without evidence of their validity." One reason why sociologists have remained content to use measures that may be of doubtful validity is that they have generally considered validity in terms of content, face, and construct validity, while ignoring questions about discriminant validity (Campbell and Fiske, 1959). For as Sechrest (1969, p. 561) emphasizes, "measures may be invalidated not only by showing that they correlate poorly with some criterion but also by showing that they correlate highly with some conceptually simpler variable, such as the tendency to respond true, or in a socially desirable manner to all items." The findings presented here and in the previous chapter call into question the discriminant validity of a number of sociological measures, as they show consistent relationships between social desirability and people's responses to various interview items.

These findings also have implications for the validity of the investigator's *results*. Many social scientists would agree that what is most important is that the undesired response determinants (such as social desirability or acquiescence) be randomly distributed among the subgroups who are being compared. Thus, for a so-called "descriptive" survey whose aim is to provide an accurate estimate of, say, the general level of happiness in the population, the effects of social desirability on the *absolute* level of happiness are clearly important. But for an "explanatory" survey, many sociologists would argue that people's distortion of their "true" feelings is unimportant, in that the research concerns the *relative* occurrence of various social phenomena in different population subgroups. Therefore, the fact that a measure of happiness or some other variable is affected by social desirability, for instance, may not matter much if all, or the members of each subgroup being compared, distort their responses in a similar manner. Consequently, following this line of reasoning, unless an unwanted response determinant is related to both the dependent variables and the independent variables of empirical interest, it will not affect the validity of the findings.

While this argument initially appears persuasive (as was mentioned in Chapter Two), it is only partially correct. It is true that the introduction of a "test factor," such as social desirability, into the analysis can only "interpret" or "explain" (Hyman, 1955) an original relationship if it is related to both the independent and dependent variables yet may still affect the relationship between them by *specifying* its direction and or magnitude or both—as was seen in Table 13. But one cannot assume (as is usually done) that any test factor will affect the dependent variable in exactly the same fashion in different segments of the population, even if it is unrelated to one's independent variable. So one cannot follow blindly the "rule of thumb" offered by Rosenberg (1968) and others that a variable has to be related to both the independent and the dependent variable of concern if it is to be used as a test factor.

In summary, if respondents' scores on various measures are related to considerations of social desirability (trait desirability or the need for social approval or both), then the validity of such measures is called into question. If social desirability is related to various measures (dependent variables) but not to the independent variables of empirical concern, social desirability may specify the direction or magnitude (or both) of the relationship between the independent and dependent variables of interest. If social desirability is related to both the dependent and independent variables, it may account for what are essentially "spurious" relationships. It is here that social desirability is probably most important for the results of sociological investigations. Given the significance of this factor, we hope the results of these analyses will stimulate further investigations into its effects in survey studies.

★★★★★★★★★★★★★★★★★★★

4

Modeling Effects: Annoyance or Bias

★★★★★★★★★★★★★★★★★★★

Another source of bias which has interested investigators is what has been termed "modeling effects." Modeling can occur when the investigator consciously or unconsciously projects his own views (attitudes, opinions, or whatever) on those whom he studies. Evidence for a modeling effect is demonstrated when there is a relationship between the behavior or responses of the investigator (laboratory experimenter, clinician, or interviewer) and the behavior or responses of those being investigated (subjects, patients, respondents). Most research on modeling effects has been conducted in psychology laboratories, although there are also studies of clinical situations and survey interviews.[1] Rosenthal (1966, pp. 125–126), who provides

[1] For laboratory studies, see Friedman (1967) and Rosenthal (1966); for clinical situations, Graham (1960) and Matarazzo and others (1965); for survey studies, Clark (1927), Hyman (1954), and Twigg (1969–1970).

an excellent review of these modeling studies, summarizes their conclusions as follows:

> *Modeling effects occur at least sometimes in psychological research conducted in field or laboratory. We find it difficult, however, to predict the direction and magnitude of modeling effects. In survey research, they tend usually to be positive but variable as to magnitude. In laboratory studies, modeling effects are variable not only in magnitude but in direction as well. The interpretation of the variability of direction of modeling effects that is best supported by the evidence, though still not established, is that a happier, more pleasant, less tense experimenter seems to model his subjects negatively. The less pleasant, more tense experimenter seems to model his subjects positively. Just why this should be is not at all clear.*

As far as can be determined, all studies of modeling effects in survey research have involved face-to-face encounters between interviewers and respondents. Therefore, modeling effects could have arisen from a variety of cues and clues in the interview procedure. For the interpersonal communication processes that mediate unintended bias are the same processes that operate in other interpersonal situations (discussed at length in Phillips, 1971). Modeling effects may come about through various kinesic and paralinguistic cues, such as shifts of posture, eye movements, gestures, and tone of voice. As Birdwhistell (1970) and others have begun to show, and as all good novelists have long known, people communicate not only by use of words but also through the use of paralinguistic, kinesic, and probably tactile, olfactory, and gustatory channels. Most of the time, words express only a portion of our meaning when we interact with other persons. Birdwhistell (pp. 157–158) estimates that "no more than 30 to 35 percent of the social meaning of a conversation or an interaction is carried on by words." Even with the audio-aural channel, people may reveal how they feel about what they say by such cues as style, tone of voice, degree of vehemence, and so on.

As part of the study on social desirability reported in Chapter Three, Clancy and I attempted to eliminate the possible influence of kinesic and other factors that may operate in face-to-face situations by restricting communication in the data-collection process to telephone interviews. More specifically, the concern was with the possible biasing effects of paralinguistic cues on the responses obtained in telephone interviews. It was hypothesized that interviewers (unintentionally and unknowingly) may convey their own views to respondents through what Trager (1958) calls "paralanguage"—which includes such factors as tempo, pitch, intensity, hesitation phenomena, and silences. In line with others who have studied modeling effects, we argue that to the extent that the responses interviewers obtain from their respondents are correlated with their own responses, we will find a bias due to modeling effects. We recognize, of course, that such a correlation is only one step in establishing a causal connection.

Methods

Although this research was intended primarily to study social desirability, it was also designed to examine the modeling effects hypothesis. In order to hold constant as many qualities of the interviewers as possible, twenty-five white female interviewers were used. All were high school graduates, between the ages of twenty-five and forty-nine, who had at least one year of experience as marketing and public opinion research interviewers. Ostensibly as a training exercise, each interviewer completed the same interview schedule that was to be administered to the respondents. Following this and prior to an examination of their responses, the interviewers were randomly assigned to the respondents. All the telephone interviews were conducted from a central location using WATS lines, and all the interviewers were supervised in a similar manner. Thus, possible variability due to having different interviewing locations and different supervisors was minimized.

To review the basic details of the study, telephone interviews were completed with a random sample of 404 adults representing all households with a listed telephone who reside in the New England and Mid-Atlantic States. (The data reported here are from the 389 respondents for whom we had complete data.) The interview schedule asked questions about general happiness, religiosity, number of friends, current health status,[2] prejudice, and doctor visits. In addition, measures of a personality construct (need for social approval), of mental health status (using the Langner inventory), and of the tendency to dissimulate (that is, to make false claims) were employed.

Because of the relatively small number of interviewers, their responses were dichotomized for each of the various measures. In most cases this technique resulted in thirteen interviewers being categorized as "high" on a given item and twelve being classified as "low"—for example, they were divided into "very happy" and "other responses." The same procedures were followed with the respondents, and Yule's Q was then used to measure the strength of association between the scores of interviewers and respondents.

Results

The correlations are all very modest in magnitude, ranging from +.17 to −.04. Although eight of the nine correlations are in the predicted direction, the relationships are obviously very weak. Still, the probability of observing eight of nine correct predictions by chance, when the chances of a correct prediction are 50/50, is less than .05. This kind of test is rather crude in that it tests for direction of modeling effects only and does not consider magnitude.[3] However, the fact that modeling effects exist at all and that there is a consistent pattern led to carrying the analysis a step further.

It is useful to examine these data in light of the controversy regarding interviewer biasing effects. Three investigations have focused on the effects of interviewer role performance on people's responses in face-to-face interviews. Although the investigators mea-

[2] The "current health status" item was substituted for "marital happiness" item (given in Chapter Three) because so few respondents were married that it was difficult to divide the "marrieds" among the twenty-five interviewers for purposes of analysis.

[3] On three other measures in the larger study there were also relationships between the responses of interviewers and respondents: acquiescence ($Q = .18$), assessment of the "social desirability" of the mental health inventory items ($Q = .08$), and assessments of the social desirability of the ten dissimulation items ($Q = .36$).

sured social distance in different ways, all three studies considered the relationship between social distance and bias. Weiss (1968) found that the smaller the social distance between interviewer and respondent, the greater the bias; Williams (1968) found that the greater the social distance, the greater the bias; and Dohrenwend and others (1968) argued that bias is greatest when social distance is both too great and too little.

In order to examine these three possibilities, we divided our respondents into three groups based on their educational attainments: those with less than twelve years of schooling, those who were high school graduates or had some college training, and those who were college graduates or had some schooling beyond college. This procedure allows modeling effects to be examined within the three education categories. Inspection of the results shown in Table 15 reveals, first of all, that the original modeling effects take a positive direction (that is, the respondents' replies are in the same direction as the interviewers') in eighteen of the twenty-four comparisons. With regard to the question of social distance between interviewers and respondents, the magnitude of the modeling effects is greatest in the highest education group for seven of the eight comparisons. The correlations range from .04 to .42. In other words, modeling effects are strongest among those respondents who are *better-educated* than the interviewers.

These results appear to support the views of Williams and of Dohrenwend and others, who see biases as related to great social distance between interviewer and respondent. However, the findings can also be seen as being in line with Weiss' argument that interviewer biasing effects are greater when there is little social distance. While objectively there is considerable social distance between the interviewers (who are all high school graduates) and the college-educated respondents, those respondents may *perceive* the interviewers as being of relatively high status and therefore similar to themselves. If this were so, it may be that college-educated respondents in some way "pay more attention" to the voice cues offered (again, it must be emphasized, unknowingly) by the interviewers than do other respondents. Or possibly the interviewers, although objectively of lower socioeconomic status than the college-educated respondents, use the language in a way more similar to

Table 15

CORRELATIONS OF RESPONSES OF INTERVIEWERS AND RESPONDENTS, BY RESPONDENTS' EDUCATION (YULE'S QS)

	Respondents' Education		
	1–11 (N = 99)	12–15 (N = 200)	16+ (N = 90)
Measures			
(a) Happiness	.24	–.12	.42
(b) Religiosity	–.08	.05	.21
(c) Number of friends	–.15	.09	.29
(d) Current health	.33	–.11	.36
(e) Prejudice	(Not examined, too few college graduates in categories of "very" and "somewhat" prejudiced)		
(f) Doctor visits	–.19	.08	.27
(g) Mental health status	.16	.02	.04
(h) Need for social approval	.03	–.09	.10
(i) Dissimulation	.16	–.04	.19

better-educated persons than to other respondents. Perhaps their training as interviewers leads them to employ a paralanguage similar to that of higher status persons.

Since the interviews were conducted by telephone, the *only* cues available to either interviewers or respondents were such things as tone of voice, modulation, and the like. The interviewers obtained *direct* knowledge about respondents' education, income, and occupation only at the very end of the telephone interview, and it seems unlikely that the interviewers in some way "modeled" their respondents. That is, since the interviewers knew nothing about the several respondents they were each to interview, they were not apt to have purposely behaved in such a manner as to obtain positively modeled responses.

The better-educated respondent, on the other hand, may be more sensitive to the cues offered by a stranger who calls him to inquire about various aspects of his life—especially if he perceives that person as of high status—than is the respondent with less education. In a sense, then, he *models himself* in line with what he takes (from the available voice cues) to be the views of the interviewer. Whether he does this to smooth the interaction, to gain approval from the interviewer by resembling him, or for some other reason is, of course, unknown. If the perceived social distance between interviewers and college-educated respondents is less than between interviewers and other respondents, then the college-educated may in some way be attracted to the interviewer because they see her as being like themselves. If this is true, then the findings in Table 15 may be viewed as evidence for Williams' (1969, p. 126) suggestion that: "If the respondent is attracted to the interviewer, he may attempt to answer questions in agreement with his perception of the interviewer's opinion in order to maintain or even increase the reward value of the interaction."

Whatever the mechanisms operating in telephone interviews, and whatever the possibly different processes operating with regard to respondents of varying educational levels, the existence of at least small modeling effects in telephone interviews has been demonstrated here.[4] Since these modeling effects are extremely small in magnitude but, still rather consistent, two conclusions might be drawn from these findings. First, because the modeling effects are such a minor source of bias, they are not worth further consideration. Therefore, one might argue that the frequent assumption that respondents are not systematically influenced by interviewers' behavior is upheld by the results presented here. An alternate conclusion, and the one we find most preferable, is as follows. If, as has

[4] Since the interviewers were all women, it might be expected that female respondents would be more subject than male respondents to the influence of "modeling effects." However, our analysis revealed only minor—and inconsistent—differences between men and women. It might also be expected that those respondents with a high need for social approval would be more influenced by interviewers' views than would those with a low need for social approval. Again, this expectation was not borne out by the data.

been found here, interviewers systematically bias respondents' reports on a variety of measures even when they are not in one another's physical presence, there may be much greater biasing effects when interviewer and respondent actually confront one another. In face-to-face communication there are many more cues available that may make modeling effects (or expectancy effects, or other sources of bias) a more major source of contamination.

A variety of factors have been found to affect the validity of the results of survey interviews. In this study we have seen at least minor influence by one source of bias—modeling effects—on people's responses to a variety of questions. While these biasing effects are admittedly small, they appear to call into question the assertion by Dohrenwend (1968, p. 122) that "Interviewers' own opinions generally are not a source of bias in respondents' answers, largely because interviewers seldom communicate their views to respondents." Obviously, the interviewer does not tell the respondent his own views, but he may unknowingly and inadvertently communicate them through paralinguistic, kinesic, and other cues. Hopefully, the findings presented here will help stimulate further investigations of the influence of modeling effects in sociological research.

★★★★★★★★★★★★★★★★★★

5

Sociology of Social Research: A Perspective

★★★★★★★★★★★★★★★★★★

That "things are not what they seem" is certainly as true for the discipline of sociology itself as for the social world which sociologists study. Recognizing this condition, an increasing number of sociologists have begun to investigate and write about what has come to be called "the sociology of sociology." These writers have turned the sociological imagination upon sociology itself, examining, among other things, the infrastructure, the organization, the assumptions, and conduct of the sociological enterprise (see, for instance, Mills, 1959; Friedrichs, 1970; Reynolds and Reynolds, 1970; and Gouldner, 1970). By and large, however, they have focused on sociological theory and have tended to neglect questions concerning the research activities of sociologists. The major critical work on these matters still remains Cicourel's book (1964), although his concern with "method and measurement" is somewhat more abstract and theoretical than mine.

I intend here to make some further observations on issues

and problems involving the collection of sociological data and to review some of my earlier views on these matters. Most of my discussion will refer to the practice of sociology in American society, both because I know it best and because I share with Gouldner (1970, p. 23) the view that "American sociology today is, for all practical purposes, the model of academic sociology throughout the world."

Validity of Interview and Questionnaire Data

Despite the heavy use of survey interviews (and questionnaires) in sociological investigations, it is not at all clear how the data obtained are relevant to the *professed* concerns of most sociologists: action, interaction, social processes, institutions, and social structures. Survey investigators typically obtain "reports" of behavior and interaction from one individual, then from another, and so on. People are grouped together on the basis of one or another variable and then discussed as if interaction, social processes, and so on had actually been observed. Thus, the use of interviews and questionnaires is often irrelevant and inappropriate to the topics being investigated. And even when they may be relevant, the results generally provide little in the way of explanatory and predictive power (for example, see Rosenthal, 1966, and Hamblin, 1966). More and more social scientists are acknowledging this lack of relevance, but what is not so often acknowledged is the fact that the results obtained are frequently invalid and inaccurate, as I argued earlier in this book (and in Phillips, 1971). Most sociologists, even if they are aware of the evidence, choose to ignore it (see, for example, Gadourek, 1972), continuing instead to devote their efforts to collecting more data, to concentrating on problems of data analysis, and to an ever increasing infatuation with mathematics and statistics. Given the demonstrably faulty quality of sociological data, these efforts are a monstrous waste of time and effort.

Data Collection as a Social Process

I have argued elsewhere (Phillips, 1971) that one of the major reasons that sociological researchers have been so unsuccessful in explaining any sizable amount of variance, and one of the reasons that their measures and findings are often invalid, is that investigators fail to recognize that the collection of social scientific data constitutes a social process. Their failure to acknowledge this is somewhat surprising. For if, as most sociologists assume, people's behavior is partially a product of their needs, values, and expectations, it should not be unexpected that their behavior (and responses) in interview situations will also be affected by these factors.

Even in the most carefully controlled laboratory experiments, psychologists have been generally unsuccessful in eliminating the influence of unwanted (biasing) factors. And Clancy and I have been equally unsuccessful in eliminating such factors in our research. Despite the fact that we followed the usual precautions for eliminating possible bias, our respondents were very much affected by considerations of social desirability. What these results indicate is that taking the usual "precautions" (following the textbook recipes) will not eliminate the influence of people's desire to place themselves in a favorable light on many measures of interest to sociological investigators.

Let me now review briefly the arguments of my earlier studies with Clancy (reported in the previous chapters) and also attempt to make explicit certain assumptions contained in our research. Our most basic assumption is that in *all* social science investigations differences among individuals on various measures reflect some, generally unknown, mixture of: (1) "true" differences in the characteristic (attitude, quality, or whatever) which the investigator is attempting to measure and (2) variations due to errors in the measurement process. It seems to me there is a great deal of evidence showing this to be the case and I will, therefore, not defend that assumption here. A second assumption is that whenever an investigator (interviewer, experimenter, observer) confronts the objects of his research interest, these individuals' responses and behavior will be affected by considerations of what is "appropriate" for someone in that kind of situation. That is, I assume that in social science investigations people tend to organize their behavior and responses in light of their "definitions of the situation"—as do people, of course, in other situations. Again the evidence is, I think, quite persuasive. (See Crowne and Marlowe, 1964; Rosenberg, 1965; and, for a somewhat different conclusion, Hermans, 1970.)

More questionable, however, are our assumptions regarding

an individual's ability to figure out the investigator's intentions, his ability to distort his "true" beliefs, feelings, behavior, and so on, and his motivations and intent for engaging in such distortions. We believe that the purposes of most self-report measures are apparent to the individual who responds to an interviewer's questioning or fills out a questionnaire. He knows (or thinks he knows, or at least hypothesizes) that what the investigator wants to know about is his mental health, sexual behavior, job satisfaction, religiosity, or whatever. He does not, we assert, merely answer questions, endorse statements, or provide data without considering the purpose of the investigation. Rosenberg (1969, p. 4), who has studied what he calls "evaluation apprehension" in psychology experiments, says that "subjects will report—sometimes with uncertainty and sometimes with great clarity—that they were burdened or preoccupied with the question 'What is the real purpose of this experiment?' " Although I know of no comparable findings from interview and questionnaire studies, I think it likely that people are almost always concerned with the purpose of the investigation.

I also believe that the implications of people's answers are rather apparent to them and that they can, and will, consciously control their responses. Again, Rosenberg's (1969, p. 19) research is recommended as evidence, although I disagree with his tentative conclusion that "subjects will usually obscure from themselves the extent to which they regulate their responding so as to win favorable judgments from the experimenter." Rather, subjects are more likely to obscure from the investigator rather than from themselves. In short, I believe that in most instances people have an idea (accurate or not) as to what is being evaluated or measured and what is the "right," "correct," or "best" response to give under the circumstances and that this idea will color their responses.

Consequences for Data Collection

What are the consequences for the ideals of social scientific research of viewing data collection as a social process?[1] This question is considered in regard to the following goals of sociological research: controlled data-collection procedures, replication of pro-

[1] The discussion in this section is taken from Phillips (1971).

cedures, and the cumulation of results. My discussion focuses mainly on survey studies and laboratory experiments, although the implications for other research techniques should be apparent.

The principal methods of data collection and analysis in survery studies and laboratory experiments have as their model the controlled experiment as found in the natural sciences. In the laboratory experiment, an "experimental" group is exposed to the independent variable of chief interest while the "control" group is not; the two groups are then compared in terms of the effects on some specified dependent variable. Randomization in assigning subjects to the two groups controls the effects of confounding variables. In studies using interviews and questionnaires, however, confounding or extraneous variables are usually controlled in one of two ways: (1) the sample is selected so that certain factors do not operate as variables (for example, only men might be included, or only persons under age forty); (2) in analyzing the data, certain variables are "held constant"; for instance, the relationship between religious affiliation and voting preference might be examined within each of several social class divisions.

In this type of controlled empirical inquiry, the ideal is that *no* variables other than those of explicit theoretical and empirical interest will affect the results. This means there should be no "uncontrolled" influences by other subject or respondent variables, situational factors, or attributes of the data collectors. Obviously, perfect control in this sense is impossible. But what is important is that unintended variations in the data-collection procedure be minor and that when unintended variations do occur, they not be systematic. In some studies of bias and invalidity, variations in the responses and behaviors of those being studied are not of minor magnitude and are related to the investigator's attributes and to such other factors as "social desirability" in a *systematic* manner—thus affecting the validity of the results.[2] These studies suggest quite clearly, I think, that much (in my view, most) social science re-

[2] Although I believed at one time (as in Phillips, 1971) that the kinds of results provided by these studies could be informative and useful in their own right as evidence of the factors operating in human interaction, I now feel that the findings cannot be generalized beyond the studies in which they have been investigated.

search falls considerably short of the ideal of controlled procedures of data collection.

Since we lack controlled data collection, it is extremely difficult to achieve the goal of replication. Though the social scientist may explicitly describe the content of the interview, the exact words that were read from the instructions by the experimenter, the way the sample was drawn, and the data analyzed, this description does not constitute replication. For if another investigator were to try to replicate the first man's data-collection procedures, he would, among other things, have to obtain interviewers (in the case of survey studies) who possessed the same relevant qualities (in the same combinations or mixes regarding their age, sex, race, expectancies, and so on) as did the original interviewers. If the intent of replication is not to vary anything which makes a systematic difference in people's responses, then replication in survey and experimental studies is much more difficult than is usually acknowledged. In fact, contrary to what is usually assumed, it may be more difficult to replicate a survey than a study based on participant observation in that conducting interviews with, say, 1000 respondents actually involves 1000 (or 999) replications of the same investigation.

Friedman's remarks (1967, p. 150) on the replication of psychological experiments are relevant here. He notes that "psychologists do not, as a rule, report how many glances they exchanged with their subjects while reading the instructions, nor would they have any way of knowing if they decided to. Nor do they, as a rule, report the exact duration of each phase of each experimental session. Hence, working from the public description of the experiment, it is unlikely that another experimenter would replicate the exchange of glances variable or the time variable." Should it be the case (as Friedman found) that the experimenter's glances are relevant to the subjects' responses and behavior, failure to include these would constitute a significant omission in a replication study. When the data-collection procedures (including all response-relevant variables in the context of the investigation) are not controlled and not reported, they are not replicable.

What can be said, then, about the third ideal: the cumulation of results? Obviously, studies based on procedures which are neither controlled nor replicable will not produce empirical results that can in some way be "added up" or built upon. The assumption by many social scientists that they can engage in research without influencing the data they obtain is without foundation. Despite the claims of many that our data collecting is objective, our procedures public, our findings replicable and cumulative, the evidence indicates the contrary.

"Research on Research"

My research with Clancy concerning social desirability is part of an increasing, but still small, number of investigations that have examined the effects of various factors operating in the collection of social science data. There are studies of modeling effects, "experimenter expectancy," and various attributes of the experimenter and interviewer. Among these are investigations showing the effects of their race (Summers and Hammonds, 1966; Williams, 1964), sex (Binder and others, 1957), age (Benney and others, 1956), religion (Robinson and Rohde, 1946), social status (Rosenthal, 1966; Lenski and Leggett, 1960), and various personality characteristics (Sampson and French, 1960; Winkel and Sarason, 1964) on the subjects of their research.

Most studies concerned with the effects of various factors as sources of bias and invalidity have not reported the proportion of variances accounted for by these factors. Rosenthal (1966), however, states that expectancy effects (the effects of experimenter expectancies on subjects' performances in laboratory research) account for at least as much variance in subjects' performances as do the effects of the main experimental variables. And Clancy and I found that the factor of social desirability accounted for more variance than did the variables of social class position and sexual status. Although I know of no relevant studies, I would hazard a guess that if we examined the combined effects of the numerous sources of bias that operate in various sociological and psychological studies we would find that they account for considerably more of the variance in the dependent variables of interest than do the major independent variables.

Those psychologists who have been most concerned with these problems have, in my opinion, been overly optimistic with regard to eliminating bias. For example, Rosenberg (1969, p. 348) states that "every investigation in this realm profits the succeeding one; error should fall away as we continue to 'zero-in' toward the goal of bias-free research." In my view, most studies of bias are themselves subject to possible biasing influences. Consider, for example, Rosenberg's studies (1969) of evaluation apprehension, the existence of which he tries to establish using post-experiment interviews. That is, after the experiment the subjects are interviewed and many report that they were concerned with trying to figure out the purposes of the experiment. Rosenberg accepts these post-experimental interviews as valid reports and fails to acknowledge that these, too, are subject to a kind of evaluation apprehension. For even after completing the experiment itself, the subject may feel he is being "evaluated" through his responses to the interviewer's questions. Consequently, he may report that he *was* concerned, because that is what he believes a "good subject" should be. On what basis can we assume that an individual's laboratory behavior will be affected by bias while his interview behavior will not?

This is not to say that laboratory researchers are totally ignorant of this problem, for they definitely are not. Orne (1968, p. 154), for example, states that "the postexperimental interview must be conducted with considerable tact and skill, creating a situation where the subject is able to communicate freely what he truly believes." The survey interview has the same goal, but reaching it is still a considerable problem. For statements like that of Orne *presume* the kind of knowledge that our investigations are designed to discover.

My research with Clancy on social desirability is subject to a similar criticism. We employed a procedure resembling that developed by Edwards and used previously by Dohrenwend. We asked each respondent to rate each item on a nine-point desirability scale. We then accepted these ratings as accurate reflections of people's perceptions of the desirability of the various items and argued that these "accurate" ratings were responsible for their giving "inaccurate" responses to the questions about mental health symptoms, religiosity, prejudice, and so on.

But, clearly, there are other possibilities. Both the desirability ratings and the responses to the various questions may be inaccurate reflections of people's "true" feelings, both may be accurate reflections, or the desirability ratings may be inaccurate while the responses to the questions are accurate. We discussed these possibilities in earlier chapters and argued that there were good theoretical reasons for preferring our line of reasoning (that the measures of social desirability were accurate and the other responses biased by social desirability) to those implied in the alternate possibilities. Yet it is difficult to demonstrate *empirically* the correctness of our position, for our attempts to discover sources of bias and invalidity in survey studies are, logically, subject to the same weakness as the measures whose validity we question.

There are two principle reasons for doing "research on research," for attempting to discover the effects of various aspects of the data-collection process on the validity of social scientists' measures and, consequently, on the validity of their results. The first is to discover the sources of error and invalidity so they can be controlled or eliminated. This clearly is the goal of most investigators who have studied bias, as is shown by the statements of writers like Rosenberg who speak of "bias-free" research. The second, which is now my position (but not that of my collaborator, Kevin Clancy), is to demonstrate the inadequacy of contemporary social science research and the impossibility of bias-free research in situations where human beings collect data from active, thinking people like themselves. For to continue to conceive of people (respondents, subjects) as "objects" who can be subjected to the control of the researcher is, in a sense, to conceive of them as "things." Gouldner (1970, p. 496) expresses this point clearly when he reminds us that "there is not as great a difference between the sociologist and those he studies as the sociologist seems to think, even with respect to an intellectual interest in knowing social worlds. Those being studied are also avid students of human relations; they too have their social theories and conduct their investigations."

Sociologist as Human Being

There is a dominant paradigm in sociology that partially defines the way a sociologist looks at social worlds and conducts his research. But the sociologist is not influenced only by the dictates of the scientific community. His own values, interests, preferences, skills, personal troubles, and biases always intrude to some extent in the selection of the best procedures for collecting data pertaining to his topic of investigation. Inevitably he chooses not only problems that concern him but also selects investigative procedures that will maximize the possibility of his finding what he is looking for or in having his hypotheses supported. For surely (as Gouldner, among others, has so clearly stated) sociology is by no stretch of the imagination value-free. An investigator's values influence not only the problem he selects for study but also his methods for studying them and the sources of data he uses.

I think it is widely recognized that all social scientists select for study the problems that interest them. No one ever should have expected anything else. But there is less recognition that their methods and sources of data are often chosen on other than the strictest scientific grounds, although this view is coming to be accepted by younger social scientists. For example, the historian Staughton Lynd (1968, 193–194) comments on his own early work as follows:

> *On the one hand it still makes sense to me that, like any other social scientist, the historian should formulate hypotheses and then test them against a restricted range of data, such as what happened in one area, or in one man's life. On the other hand I am now more conscious that I selected a range of data that I could be relatively certain would substantiate a thesis that I hoped was true. I studied opposition to the United States Constitution in Dutchess County, New York, because Dutchess County has a history of landlord-tenant conflict very likely to be connected with how groups aligned themselves for or against the ratification of the Constitution. The bias involved in my selection of Dutchess County did not necessarily invalidate my findings, but it raised serious questions as to their generalability. I believe this is how bias characteristically operates in the work of other historians, too: not in deliberate mishandling of evidence, but in selection of research design.*

I suspect that what Lynd indicates about data used to test his own thesis is equally true for the vast majority of social science investigations.

However, there is another aspect of the investigator's influence that remains widely ignored and, in fact, has only recently begun to receive the attention it deserves. I refer here to the investigator's implicit theories of human behavior and his assumptions that guide and, to a large extent, probably determine the outcome of his research activities. Although many seem reluctant to admit it, sociologists—like all other men—view the behavior of themselves and others in terms of certain assumptions about humankind, about society, and about men and women in interaction with one another. And social researchers organize their research and their writings in terms of such prior assumptions. It could not be otherwise, for like those whom they study and write about, sociologists are influenced by their own experiences. Some undoubtedly will argue that they make no assumptions about men and society or that their assumptions are "supported by empirical evidence." In my view, this is nonsense. Whether we see men as self-centered or altruistic, whether we see them as possessing free will or not, and what we see as their basic "needs," for example, are not determined by reference to principles of social behavior and interaction. A fundamental problem in sociology is that what we know about social behavior (and, indeed, most social phenomena) is dependent on our methods for studying it, while our methods for studying it depend on what we know about social behavior. So in order to know more about social behavior and interaction, we need better methods; and to obtain better methods, we need to know more about behavior and interaction. This constitutes a kind of vicious circle which we must break out of if the social sciences are to move beyond their present stage of development.

Clearly, the fact that we have neither adequate methodologies nor basic principles of social behavior has not prevented sociologists from theorizing about social phenomena or from engaging in empirical research. They are able to proceed because they are guided by *some* view of men, both with regard to their nature and to the ways they operate as social actors. As I noted, these views are seldom made explicit—although they can easily be seen in the myriad "interpretations" which different sociologists offer in an attempt to make sense of the results of various studies. Given the task of explaining some pattern of association between two variables, different sociologists would be unlikely to agree on an explanation.

This being the case, it is not at all surprising that there should be great differences among sociologists in the factors chosen to explain various social phenomena. Some of these differences are due to different orientations among different subareas of sociology, which are often concerned with different concrete subject matter. Even when the phenomena to be explained are similar, sociological practitioners will select different causal or determining factors. This is, perhaps, to be expected in that the various subareas have a long history of different concerns, emphases, and traditions. But even within a particular subspecialty, a tremendous number of factors are chosen to explain the phenomena of interest. In sociological research, the range of possible variables is so great—including both structural and social psychological variables—that investigators can choose from a seemingly infinite universe of possibilities. And since there are no formal scientific criteria to govern their selection, the choice is often based on the individual investigator's own feelings, hunches, preferences, or whatever. In short, his own experience dictates what variables he selects, although he may pay lip service to the literature and to various models and theoretical perspectives.

I would like now to return to the "vicious circle" quality of the interdependence between theory and methods: in order to know more about social behavior and interaction, we need better methods and data; while to acquire better methods and data, we need to know more about behavior and interaction. So, for example, to eliminate error from our research, we require certain kinds of knowledge about behavior and interaction that will tell us where and why errors may arise. In short, we require agreed-upon principles of social behavior and interaction. At present, these principles are lacking. The objective of using various methods in doing research is to discover such principles. But research is a social activity and, therefore, is affected by the very principles which we have not yet discovered or not yet agreed upon. And so it goes, in a vicious circle.

I have puzzled over this dilemma at length in an attempt to make some judgment about where our priority lies—with theory or with methods and research. My conclusion is neither the pluralistic view that we need both, nor Coleman's view (1969, p. 106) that "innovations in methods are urgently required," but rather that in most sciences the major changes and advances come not through new research technique or new data but from new ways of looking at existing data (Kuhn, 1962; Polanyi, 1958).

Thus the answer—if there is an answer—lies with new theories and new conceptual schemes, with radical conceptual breaks or discontinuities. But in reaching this conclusion I have reformulated both my notion of data and the idea of theory as it is usually thought of in sociology. With regard to data, I do not mean that we must look more closely at only (or necessarily) the kinds of data that are *purposively* collected in empirical investigations employing interviews and questionnaires or other research "techniques." Rather, I mean we must try to look at the world through our own eyes and not through our "scientific" instruments that frequently cloud our vision or blind us entirely. By theory I do not mean the activities engaged in by such writers as Parsons, Merton, Homans, or Zetterberg but the primordial conception of theorizing that originated with the pre-Socratics: the idea of theorizing as a self-conscious and reflexive activity. (For excellent sociological examples, see Blum, 1970a and 1970b, and Blum and McHugh, 1971.) In a very profound sense, we must take ourselves and our own experiences more seriously than we do at present. But we must go further. We must become more self-conscious about how we organize and use our ideas. We must consider what we "know" and treat that as a problem.

Starting from a somewhat different vantage point, Gouldner (1970) reaches a similar conclusion. And although he has expressed his view with clarity and passion, there are those who ask to be shown "how." What they are asking for, I believe, is a set of directions as to how to think and how to live their lives. Alas, there are no ready answers to such questions. But sociologists who fail to consider these questions are clearly not alive to life. Perhaps they are asleep. If so, it is our obligation to awaken them.

★★★★★★★★★★★★★★★★★

6

Warranting Knowledge

★★★★★★★★★★★★★★★★★

Every scientific discipline faces the problem of deciding what is to be accepted as constituting knowledge. Its practitioners must generally agree on the criteria which, for that group and that time, determine what is regarded as scientific knowledge. In the scientific world today it seems to be true, as Habermas (1971, p. 67) laments, that "knowledge is implicitly defined by the achievement of the sciences." Thus, sociological knowledge is found, for example, in Berelson and Steiner's inventory (1964, p. 27) of factual findings, containing "what is more or less proved about human behavior." In addition, of course, sociological knowledge is to be found in sociological journals, textbooks, and research monographs.

A central thesis of this chapter[1] is that the structure of

[1] I wish to thank Irwin Deutscher and Lionel Lewis for their helpful comments on an earlier draft of this chapter. I am especially indebted to Alan Blum, who has allowed me to draw freely on his unpublished manuscript "The Problem of Warrant: Sociological Procedures for Deciding the Factual Status of Findings," which provided the inspiration and beginning

science can be defined in terms of the procedural rules which determine what sets of propositions are considered to constitute the corpus of science at a given time. In the following pages I discuss some of the procedural rules used by sociologists (and recognized and utilized by the sociological community) to determine whether what their propositions or statements propose is to be accepted as factual knowledge. In conceiving of a fact as a proposition which is assigned a certain status, I assume—like writers as diverse as Kuhn (1962, 1970a), Winch (1958), and Kaufman (1958)—that the entire problem involved in ascertaining fact is organized around a concern with the user's rules of procedure, rather than with the "essential" quality of some thing in nature. As McHugh (1970, p. 332) so clearly states: "nothing—no object, event, or circumstance—determines its own status as truth, either to the scientist or to science. . . . [A]n event is transformed into the truth only by the application of a canon of procedure, a canon that truth-seekers use and analysts must formulate as providing the possibilty of agreement." In other words, *we do not consult what a proposition proposes, we consult the rules used to decide if what the proposition proposes is warranted.*

Thus, the proposition "the greater the interaction, the greater the liking" is not accepted or rejected on the basis of asking whether interaction *really* leads to liking (for where would we look to find out?), but by asking what rules of procedure one should use to decide whether such a proposition can be accredited as fact. Similarly, with the statement "a higher percentage of Protestants than Jews vote the Democratic ticket," we ask for the sociological rules of procedure that lead to the acceptance or rejection of this statement. Before I consider the various procedural rules in sociology, let me turn briefly to the matter of sociological knowledge and to a consideration of why I regard procedural rules as at the heart of all science.

While there is not, as we know, complete agreement among sociologists as to what constitutes sociological "knowledge," there does appear to be consensus among investigators that the corpus of

---

for this essay. Conversations with him have led me to revise some of my earlier views (as in, for example, Phillips, 1971).

sociological knowledge consists of a collection of bona fide statements of empirical regularities involving social phenomena. But how are "bona fide" propositions determined? What are the criteria for judging whether statements are to be accepted into this body of knowledge? Although sociologists continually refer to a collection of warranted propositions which they appear to trust and respect as factual knowledge, there is surprisingly little discussion in the methodological literature about how findings come to be accepted as factual or bona fide. Merton (1957) speaks of "organized skepticism," a process whereby a potential candidate for admission to a scientific corpus of knowledge is subjected to careful scrutiny; and Storer (1966, p. 119) notes that contributions to scientific knowledge are always subjected to what he calls a "certification process." Yet, the criteria used for warranting findings are not clearly defined in sociology. I do not deny that sociologists disagree as to which particular factual propositions constitute basic knowledge. But this disagreement should not obscure the point that all sociological inquiry is nevertheless directed toward discovering, endorsing, or integrating factual propositions.

It is important to consider briefly here the notion of a fact, since concern with facts seems to be central to all science and to most conceptions of knowledge.[2] In most dictionary definitions of knowledge, the words *fact* or *facts* occur with some frequency. In other writing *fact* refers to both things and propositions. The first usage can be seen in Brodbeck's definition (1959, p. 377): "A 'fact' is a particular thing, characteristic, event, or kind of event, like Johnny's I.Q., or the proportion of homeowners, or the size of the Republican vote. To state a fact, then, is to state that a concept has an instance or a number of instances." The second usage of the word offers a statement or assertion about the factual nature of propositions. These may be in the form "the greater the interaction, the greater the liking" or "a higher percentage of Protestants than Jews vote the Democratic ticket." This broader usage can be seen, for instance, in Nettler's statement (1970, p. 87) that "true statements, alternatively called 'facts,' are, for the scientist, propositions about phenomena verifiable by reference to publicly replicable and

[2] For a contrary view of what constitutes "knowledge," see Habermas (1970).

communicable experiences." As is known, the positivists of the late nineteenth century assumed that facts have an intrinsic nature and that science was a matter of uncovering the "facts of nature" and reporting on what was immediately observable and measurable. This early view has come to be rejected, and the emphasis is now on collecting data in terms of their theoretical relevance. In the case of sociology, this means that investigators are encouraged to be explicit about the propositions they are testing (Gamberg, 1969). Thus, my concern here is with facts as statements or propositions rather than with facts as things.

Returning now to the question of how a proposition is accredited as factual or not, it is obvious that such a decision cannot be made by referring to some "object" or preestablished structure that corresponds to the proposition, as some positivists would have it. For as McHugh (1970, p. 327) points out: "The object-determined standard requires of shared or common truth that each observer be located in precisely the same position—physically, psychologically, socially—vis-a-vis the object. Otherwise, observers would have a different line on the object, and, therefore, be receiving different signals." Nor are decisions made by referring to such independent sources as the Bible, a catalogue of "established facts," or to a handbook of sociological "laws," such as one might expect to find in physics or chemistry. Rather, and this is a point to which sociologists pay insufficient attention, propositions are placed into either of two disjunctive classes in accordance with rules of procedure in the various sciences.

These rules are not God-given, but represent some degree of consensus within the sociological community. The importance of consensus in science is emphasized by Thomas Kuhn in *The Structure of Scientific Revolutions,* in which he introduces the notion of shared "paradigm" which commits those in a scientific discipline to the same rules and standards for scientific practice. Such paradigms "provide scientists not only with a map but also with some of the directions for map-making. In learning a paradigm the scientist acquires theory, methods, and standards together, usually in an inextricable mixture" (1962, p. 108). The importance of Kuhn's argument is to remind us that science is a *social* enterprise, with an organized consensus of men determining what is and is not science, and what is and is not to be warranted as knowledge. Of course, in sociology, as in every other science, the criteria for certifying knowledge are affected by the world view and praxis of the ruling group within the discipline (Gouldner, 1970; Kuhn, 1962; Polanyi, 1958; Weigert, 1970).

It is not my intention here to examine how particular rules have come to be given and accepted. Rather I devote most of my attention to findings resulting from studies using interviews and questionnaires, as these are the most heavily used data-collection methods in sociological research (Webb and others, 1966; Brown and Gilmartin, 1969). I also mention briefly the procedural rules used to warrant statements resulting from participant observation studies.

Procedural Rules

Though procedural rules are examined in almost every methodology textbook in sociology, the most explicit discussion of accrediting sociological propositions is found in Zetterberg (1966, pp. 110–111). Since he treats these rules in a much more systematic matter than do other sociologists dealing with the same materials, it is convenient to use Zetterberg's criteria in my discussion of the the various rules. I emphasize, however, that these rules do not originate with Zetterberg and are not peculiar to him.

Zetterberg offers the following as the relevant criteria in "confirming a proposition":

(1) the validity of the indicators; (2) the reliability of the indicators; (3) the fit between the data trend from the indicators and the trend predicted by the tested proposition: (a) the extent to which the direction of the trends coincide; (b) the likelihood that the data trend is a chance fluctuation; (4) the control of alternative propositions; (5) the representativeness of the sample and the scope of the population; and (6) the extent to which the tested proposition is an integral part of established theory.

He also states (p. 110) that "all these criteria have to be weighted into a composite judgment of acceptance or rejection." I now turn to an examination of these criteria, these rules of procedure, for deciding on the factual status of an investigator's results.

In doing so, I shall be concerned with the manner and extent to which investigators pay attention to the criteria listed above.

Reliability and Validity of Indicators. Whether a proposition or statement is accepted as factual is considered to be partly dependent on the reliability and validity of the indicators used to measure it. Reliability refers to the extent to which a measuring instrument is likely to yield a consistent result. Selltiz and others (1959, p. 148) define reliability as follows: "independent but comparable measures of the same object (or attitude, or whatever) should give similar results (provided, of course, that there is no reason to believe that the object being measured has in fact changed between the two measurements)." Zetterberg notes that the term is used in several different ways, but defines reliability as (1966, p. 123) "the extent to which an indicator renders unambiguous readings." Validity, on the other hand, refers to whether a measure, in fact, measures what it purports to measure (Cannell and Kahn, 1968). Or, according to Zetterberg (p. 114), "validity, loosely speaking, is the extent to which an indicator corresponds to a definition." In other words, a measuring instrument is judged valid when its results are deemed comparable with other relevant evidence.

Despite the heavy emphasis on reliability and validity in methodological textbooks, they are seldom given detailed attention in the actual research activities of sociologists. Reliability is occasionally mentioned, but questions of validity are almost completely ignored.[3] Zetterberg points out that measures are valid only to the extent that they are accurately reported. "Lack of validity because of false information is, in principle, possible to detect. In practice, however, it is very troublesome" (p. 123). That is undoubtedly true, yet there does exist—as I have indicated in earlier chapters—a great deal of evidence as to the invalidity of much sociological data. Even though the validity can often be checked against outside criteria, and even though many measures can be examined in terms of their discriminant validity, few sociological measures are actually

[3] Deutscher (1969) claims that the problem of validity has been generally neglected in the social sciences, while Ajzen and others (1970) state that there is a vast literature regarding validity. It seems to me that there is, indeed, a rather large body of literature on the subject in psychology but almost nothing of substance in sociology.

validated. When attempts are made to validate certain measures, the results are frequently ignored by subsequent investigators. Despite the evidence presented by Clark and Tifft (1966), for instance, on self-reports of delinquency, a recent study of self-reported delinquency makes no mention of the possible invalidity of its measures (Hindelang, 1971), although the Clark and Tifft study is cited. Similarly, both Dohrenwend's research and my own studies with Clancy on social desirability as a source of bias are ignored in the subsequent research of such investigators as Summers and others (1971), though they indicate awareness of these earlier studies. And, of course, Douglas' book on suicide (1967) has not dissuaded sociologists from blindly following the path of Durkheim's work on the subject.

In summary, while there is much talk of the importance of validity and reliability as crucial criteria (that is, procedural rules) for accepting or rejecting sociological propositions in research, they are seldom reported in the results of empirical investigations. When they are reported, they sometimes cast doubt on the validity of many of our measures, but then they are frequently ignored by future investigators. Since invalid and unreliable indicators are thought to lead to the discrediting of sociological propositions, it is remarkable that they are not taken more seriously by investigators in their research. This failure makes Zetterberg's criteria of validity and reliability rather mysterious as procedural rules to be considered in the warranting of sociological propositions.

Fit Between Data Trend and Predicted Trend. Here Zetterberg (p. 110) speaks of "the extent to which the direction of the trends coincide," and "the likelihood that the data trend is a chance fluctuation." These can be determined by examining measures of the strength of association, in the first case, and tests of significance in the second.

Although in recent years there has been a considerable increase in the reporting of measures of association, there are still numerous studies in which they are not reported at all. When they are reported, the strength of the relationship between the chief independent and dependent variables is such that the independent variable seldom accounts for more than 10 to 15 percent of the variance in the dependent variable. Depending more than anything else, I suspect, on whether the work in question is one's own or someone else's, this strength is variously described as "fully" or "only" 10 percent, 15 percent, or whatever. The important point here is that there are no agreed upon standards in the sociological community that allow one to determine how to regard relationships of varying strengths.

Perhaps partially because of this lack of criteria, the most heavily used procedural rule in sociology is the test of significance, which tries to find out how often differences of magnitude could have occurred as chance fluctuations in sampling. Thus, the proposition "the greater the interaction, the greater the liking" is taken as factual or warranted when the findings can be shown to differ "significantly" from what the proposition excludes—that greater interaction does not lead to greater liking. Of course, the investigator is expected to establish in advance what degree of difference between what a proposition proposes and what it excludes he is willing to accept as a criterion for acceptance or rejection of his proposition. Usually the .05 or .01 level of significance is accepted, and the rule of procedure invoked by the investigator is summarized in a table of probability values and in the logic of statistical inference.

I will not consider here the rather sizable literature concerning this rule of procedure, except to note that conventions for deciding statistical significance are based on what Dunnette (1966) terms a "foundation of triviality." With moderately large samples, many comparisons will yield statistically significant results. When these results are accompanied by inconsequential correlations, the investigator's attention and subsequent discussion are almost invariably focused on the "significance" of the results rather than on the strength of correlation. Although Zetterberg stresses that this procedure should be considered together with the other procedural rules, it is not at all clear how this goal is to be accomplished. Consequently, the "rule of statistical inference" is appealed to more than any other procedural rule in deciding whether or not to accept a proposition as factual.

Control of Alternative Propositions. Zetterberg observes (p. 141) that "the problem of the ruling-out of alternative hypotheses is known as the problem of 'control' in a verification enterprise. We should distinguish between the control of known alternative hypotheses and the control of unknown alternative hypotheses. The best method of verification controls both known and unknown alternatives. A method of this extraordinary kind does exist and is known as the 'experimental' design." Many social scientists emphasize that the method of experiment presents the most powerful means yet devised to test hypotheses and to establish causality. The experimental design, as Zetterberg notes, "controls alternatives by producing the hypothesized determinant and by randomization of known and unknown factors. The experimenter does not merely observe what his hypothesis assumes as the determinant, but, in addition, himself produces it" (p. 141).

Those who have written about the advantage of the experiment stress the feature of "control" (Festinger, 1953, pp. 136–173; Skinner, 1947, pp. 16–50). Morgan (1956, p. 12), for instance, has stated that "the experiment is . . . important to science because it provides control. One trouble with casual or natural observation is that we cannot be sure of the conditions that might give us misleading results." Control is obviously the ideal, but as Rosenthal (1966) and Friedman (1967), among others, have shown, it is not so simply accomplished in laboratory experiments in psychology. Such influences as experimenter effects and variability in experimental procedures introduce bias and invalidity. Even the most carefully controlled laboratory experiments cannot eliminate sources of bias that arise in the interaction between subject and experimenter or between subject and setting. Thus many laboratory psychologists now recognize that the control and standardization which have born fruit in the climate of the physical and natural sciences cannot so easily be transplanted to the psychological experiment.

It is even more difficult to achieve control in most sociological studies which do not involve experimental procedures. In most sociological investigations, control comes about in two ways: by selecting the sample so that certain factors do not operate as variables and by holding constant certain variables in the analysis of the data. Achievement of control is one of the major purposes of the techniques of multivariate analysis pioneered by Lazarsfeld. "The technique controls alternative propositions by testing the hypothesis in subsamples that are homogeneous with respect to the determinants specified by the alternative propositions. It can be used to control all known alternative determinants, provided the sample used is large enough" (Zetterberg, 1966, p. 144). Concern for controlling alternative propositions can also be seen in the use of path analysis.

When an investigator has obtained initial support for his proposition (in the ideal case because he has demonstrated the reliability and validity of his measures, has discovered a "significant" relationship, and has found a correlation of "some strength"), he then tries to show that his proposition is not a specific instance of other propositions (or the effect of other variables). Even with the development of new statistical procedures, the possibility of looking at other variables in various combinations is always limited by the size of the sample and by the amount of computer time he can afford.

The researcher in examining alternative explanations is using a version of Popper's "falsification" strategy (1959) because he takes the difference generated by the original proposition (between what it proposes and excludes) and says that he will call what it proposes warranted or a fact if the difference persists in the face of repeated and strong tests (consisting of the introduction of competing propositions).[4] However, it is important to emphasize that the introduction of such alternative propositions is largely a function of the investigator's skill in conceiving possible "tests" and of the character of his research instrument, which can only yield certain types of information. So, for example, many psychologists who conduct laboratory investigations might (following the results of Rosenthal, 1966; Rosenberg, 1965b; Friedman, 1967; and Orne, 1969) as part of their research collect data regarding such biasing factors as expectancy effects and evaluation apprehension. Most sociological investigators would be certain to collect data on age, sex, social class, and other factors that have previously been found "relevant." But the investigator cannot specify the universe of possible alternative propositions (or variables) that he has considered or how he decided to include measures of some but not others. Thus, the chief criticism of the procedural rule on controlling vari-

[4] Falsification is considered at length in the following chapter,

ables is that the investigator never makes explicit the rules of his search for relevant variables or his rules for choice among them.

Although it is not mentioned by Zetterberg, another related procedural rule that has come to be championed among some social scientists is the use of multiple measures. The possible utility of this procedure has been stressed by Webb and others (1966, pp. 173–174): "If no single measurement class is perfect, neither is any scientifically useless . . . for the most fertile research for validity comes from a combined series of different measures, each with its idiosyncratic weakness, each pointed to a single hypothesis. When a hypothesis can survive the confrontation of a series of complementary methods of testing, it contains a degree of validity unattainable by one tested within the more constricted framework of a single method." One difficulty with multiple methods is that there are no stated criteria by which one can decide how to regard inconsistent findings. If a survey should provide one pattern of results, observations another, and an experiment still another, how is one to decide which result to accept? A more serious question about multiple methods concerns the rationale underlying their use. Denzin (1970, p. 27), for example, states that "the combination of multiple measures—each with their own bias, true—into a single investigation will better enable the sociologist to forge valid propositions that carefully consider relevant causal factors." The argument that several biased measures considered together will yield more valid propositions than any of them considered alone is a bit hard to understand. It is apparently assumed that the various biases will in some way cancel one another out, rather than exercise an additive effect on the results. In fact, it seems clear that if enough were known about the sources and magnitudes of the various biases to enable an investigator to talk about combining methods (and biases), his knowledge would probably be sufficient to allow him to either control for or eliminate them. The problem is that this kind of knowledge is usually lacking and therefore the usefulness of multiple methods to establish propositions and to control or eliminate alternative propositions is not as apparent as its advocates seem to believe.

Representativeness of Sample and Scope of Population. Representativeness as a criterion for accepting a proposition as factual is one to which sociologists usually do pay a good deal of attention, especially in sampling, and as Zetterberg (1966, p. 128) observes: "Sociologists in general seem to have a very advanced conception of the role of samples in research." That is, they generally agree about the "proper" procedures for drawing, for example, a random sample from some universe, although there is perhaps less agreement regarding a representative sample. A more serious difficulty involves the universe from which samples are to be drawn, for a complete description of the boundaries and characteristics of the universe is seldom available. This issue is dealt with in various ways by sociologists: sometimes the problem of the adequacy of the sampling universe is ignored, sometimes it is argued that this is the most "adequate" sampling universe available, and frequently it is given only brief mention—as in the statement (Mitchell, 1971, p. 20) that "individuals eighteen years of age and over were the ultimate sampling units in this multistage sampling plan." Generally, however, many sociological investigations contain an explicit statement regarding the type of sample selected and the sampling universe from which it was drawn.

The scope of the population is a more serious problem, for, as Zetterberg (1966, p. 127) notes, "most theorizing claims universality." To be consistent with such aims one might expect that sociologists would strive for samples selected from all men, all women, all blacks, or whatever. Because such a sample is not feasible sociologists settle for one that is thought to be representative of all men or women, or whatever, in Detroit, in the freshman class at Midwest University, in firms A, B, and C, and so forth. Most populations selected for study are necessarily of limited scope. This limitation does not seem particularly bothersome to sociological researchers, and one frequently finds in the presentation of empirical findings statements put forth as if they should be considered universal in scope.

What is important to recognize here is that considerations of representativeness and scope can sometimes not be easily dealt with by appealing to some set of recognized and fixed standards. That is, though these factors are used as procedural rules for warranting sociological propositions, the way they are utilized is often vague and unclear.

Tested Proposition as Integral Part of Established Theory. About this last procedural rule sociologists have least to say, yet it is, in my judgment, the most problematic with respect to the warranting of sociological propositions. This step of Zetterberg's judges a proposition as fact on the basis of another, presumably "theoretic" proposition existing at the time of the decision. He says (p. 107) we must ask: "How well integrated is the tested proposition in available social theory?" We must be concerned, he says, with whether the proposition is consistent with other confirmed propositions. The problem here is with what constitutes "consistency" as well as with the tremendous variability in conceptions of accredited propositions (that is, their identity) at the time of the decision.

These "confirmed" propositions are used in various ways. In what is perhaps the most prevalent case, the investigator states some proposition and then searches for accepted propositions which can serve as grounds for assigning factual status to his proposition. Thus, after stating propositions about social stratification, political man, or whatever, the sociologist will try to discover in certain records, or previous studies, or the general body of knowledge propositions which support his new ones. But the investigator never makes explicit the rules of his search and rarely states the conditions under which he may be counted wrong.

Consider, for example, Kornhauser's monograph (1959) on the politics of mass society, and note the way he assigns factual status to new propositions. "Among countries that have already experienced considerable industrial development, those that have made the greatest progress in raising the standard of living for the bulk of the population have produced the stronger democracies, whereas those countries that have experienced less progress possess the greater anti-democratic tendencies." He assigns factual status to this proposition on the basis of a 1949 table which shows an inverse correlation between per capita income and the percentage of the vote obtained by Communist parties in certain countries (p. 169).

Another proposition he puts forth is: "Workers who are socially isolated manifest the greater susceptibility to mass tendencies" (p. 220). This proposition he assigns factual status on the following grounds: (1) a survey showing political extremism among workers in mining and maritime industries; (2) data showing the political extremism of workers isolated by prolonged unemployment; (3) data showing that unskilled workers as compared to skilled workers have weaker social ties and weaker commitment to democratic values; and (4) data showing that German, French, and Italian workers with high skilled and better paying jobs are more likely to express preference for democratic institutions.

Kornhauser's book aptly illustrates my point: without telling the reader how they have gone about accepting some propositions and rejecting others, sociologists often assign factual status to new propositions because these propositions are viewed as concurring in meaning or sense with already accepted propositions—those which are members of the corpus of knowledge at the time of the decision.

Sometimes, of course, sociologists do try to review all the evidence relevant to the propositions they advance. Rogers and Shoemaker (1971), for example, advance a series of generalizations and cite studies both supporting and not supporting each of them. One proposition is: "Earlier knowers of an innovation have higher social status than later knowers" (p. 108). As evidence they state that eighteen studies support the proposition while ten do not. Apparently, then, assessing the relevant evidence is a completely democratic affair, based on majority rule. Whether the studies located are published or unpublished, based on large samples or small ones, with or without reports of the validity or reliability of the indicators, and without mentioning whatever other differences there might be among them, they are all treated as "equal" when it comes to judging whether or not a proposition is warranted. So long as more than half of the studies located are seen as consistent with the proposition, it is taken as warranted. One could demand that the proposition be supported by two-thirds, or three-quarters, or any other proportion one chooses to select. The point, though, is that the investigator must rely on a common-sense rule for determining what is an "adequate" level of support for his proposition.

A related question is, what constitutes a "relevant" study? Rogers and Shoemaker include in their list of studies supporting their proposition ("Earlier knowers of an innovation have higher social status than later knowers"), for instance, a study by Spitzer and Denzin (1965). This latter study was conducted during the ten hours following the initial report that President Kennedy had been shot, and, among other things, the 151 respondents were asked "four open-end questions regarding the assassination: (1) Where did it happen? (2) When did it happen? (3) How did it happen? and (4) Who did it?" (p. 235). Based on their replies to these four questions, respondents were assigned a total score for the amount of "correct" information they had. On the page in Spitzer and Denzin (p. 236) cited by Rogers and Shoemaker as relevant to *their* proposition, it is reported that "analysis of the low-informed segment by occupation showed that while blue collar workers represented only 12 percent of the high-informed segment, they made up a significantly greater portion, 30 percent, of the low-informed segment. . . . Analysis of the low-informed segment by residential area disclosed that low-knowers were significantly underrepresented in the neighborhood with highest housing values."

In other words, these findings by Spitzer and Denzin are interpreted by Rogers and Shoemaker as supporting their proposition that "earlier knowers of an innovation have higher social status than later knowers." I am not arguing that their citation of the Spitzer-Denzin study is mistaken or incorrect, but rather that we are not told the rules by which they are able to transform one or another set of findings into support for their proposition. Again, the point is that some kind of commonsensical, taken-for-granted procedure is used.

In the preceding discussion, the accepted propositions which investigators chose to support their new propositions were so-called empirical generalizations. These are not the only types of warranting statements used, however. Sometimes the "confirmed" propositions are more abstract and "theoretical." For example Cloward and Ohlin (1960) propose the following proposition as factual: "Delinquency is the result of the failure of lower class youth to reduce the discrepancy between culturally induced aspirations and possibilities of achieving these aspirations through legitimate means." As closely as can be determined from the text, Cloward and Ohlin appear to warrant this proposition on the following grounds: (1) all youths internalize the same aspirations; (2) lower class youths are not in an advantageous structural position for realizing such aspirations; (3) there is a discrepancy between what lower class youth want and what they are capable of achieving; (4) this discrepancy can be (a) accepted and lived with, (b) conventionally reduced, or (c) illegitimately reduced; and (5) lower class youths who are not identified as delinquent have taken solution (a) or (b) or both. These warranting propositions are different from those in the examples from Kornhauser or Rogers and Shoemaker because the propositions serving as grounds for the warranting rule are not previously established empirical relationships but appear to be general, theoretical propositions which are presumably part of the sociological corpus of knowledge.

It should be emphasized that in all these examples, Kornhauser and Rogers and Shoemaker as well as Cloward and Ohlin, the sociologists' conception of what is an accepted proposition at the time of his decision—in the absence of his creation of such a proposition—is, in a very real sense, based on a "common-sense" rule for assigning factual status. The grounds tend to be that "anybody knows" that such-and-such a proposition is an accepted part of the corpus of knowledge. In the case of Kornhauser, any "study" which can be defined in such a way as to corroborate the new proposition is regarded as equivalent to an accepted proposition. Rogers and Shoemaker also define corroborating studies as equivalent to an accepted proposition, but they also require that the majority of relevant studies support the new proposition. Using these strategies, a sociologist apparently warrants new propositions as factual if he can locate "old" studies as evidence. These old studies then immediately acquire the status of accredited propositions in the body of knowledge, their warrant consisting only and exclusively of the fact that the investigator needs them to support his own new proposition.

On the other hand, Cloward and Ohlin did not locate previous studies to warrant their proposition but drew on the core of common-sense knowledge of the discipline, which they presumed to be accredited by members. In the examples of Kornhauser and of Rogers and Shoemaker, studies redefined as empirical propositions are used as grounds; while in the case of Cloward and Ohlin a number of notions which sociologists trust, believe, and have faith in are restated so as to appear to have factual status in the discipline.

This sixth procedural rule for warranting propositions is

very different from the other five. First, while the other rules cited are all usually used as grounds for deciding the factual status of statements created by the investigator, the warranting rule just discussed does not summarize relations between indicator events which he has produced. Second, using the sixth rule, the investigator is not able to statistically control the difference between what the proposition proposes and what it excludes and is hard put to make a quantitative determination of this difference or to state the criteria necessary for him to be counted wrong. The power of the rule, of course, lies in the fact that it enables the investigator to approach a wider range of problems than he could ordinarily handle if he operated only under the conception of fact embedded in the first five procedural rules for warranting a proposition.

Procedural Rules in Participant Observation

Although participant observation is not as frequently used as interviews and questionnaires, I consider it important to say something about the procedural rules most commonly followed by anthropological field workers and participant observers. Fortunately, a frequently cited article by Becker (1958) summarizes the sort of considerations which are typically taken into account in assigning factual status in such situations.

Let us assume that the investigator submits some proposition that summarizes his sense of an aspect of the situation he is investigating. By asking how he determines whether his proposition is factual, we are inquiring into the way he arrives at his decision. On what basis is fact assigned to the proposition "first-year medical students have orientation X?" Becker (1958, p. 656–657) gives the following grounds. (1) Each member of the group said in response to a direct question that this was how he looked at the matter. (2) Each member of the group volunteered to an observer that he viewed the matter in the same way. (3) Some given proportion of the group's members either answered a direct question or volunteered the information that they shared this perspective, but none of the others either volunteered the statement or were asked about it. (4) Every member of the group was asked or volunteered information but some given proportion said they viewed the matter from a different perspective. (5) No one was asked or volunteered but all were observed to engage in behavior or to make other statements from which the analyst inferred that such-and-such was the case. (6) Some given proportion of the group was observed in such a way, but the rest of the group was not so observed. (7) Some proportion of the group was observed to be engaged in activities implying such-and-such, while the remainder was observed as engaged in activities implying the exact opposite.

Thus, the first two grounds assign factual status because every member indicates verbally that the proposition is acceptable. In our terms, this means that all members of the group indicate by word that they agree with what the proposition proposes. Note, however, that the investigator infers that his subjects' reports of their agreement with what the proposition proposes is not couched in reference to what the proposition excludes. By not forcing the subjects to compare what the proposition proposes with what it excludes, he assumes that subjects' agreement with what the proposition proposes is equivalent to disagreeing with what the proposition excludes. It appears that in these cases the goal is only to establish whether what the proposition proposes is to be warranted without reference to what the proposition excludes. Clearly, the assumption is that if no one mentions what the proposition excludes it is not as important; and the assumption gains strength from the fact that every member of the group is responsive in this case.

From here on, however, things become more problematic. The third and fourth grounds are based on the fact that while a number of members indicate agreement with what the proposition proposes, other members agree with what the proposition excludes (orientation Y or orientation Z), in one case, and in the other case they are not asked. Clearly, in order to warrant the proposition in these cases, the investigator must make use of some rule that *weights* the responses of members so that he may say that all those who disagree with the proposition are in some sense atypical of the group or that the opinions of those who were not asked are reflected in the opinions of those who indicated agreement.

Ground five describes the typical case of inferring concepts events from behavioral indicator events and the warranting rule is based on the theory of meaning that the investigator uses to relate the two sets of events. Grounds six and seven again require the investigator to invoke a rule which weights the representativeness of subjects and of the situations. Because the inference is derived from observing some members engaged in *some* activities which are taken to document the existence of orientation X, it is clear that any assignment of fact must clarify the nature of the membership as representative and the nature of the action as adequate evidence.

If, as in the cases of the general procedural rules discussed earlier, all of these seven grounds required for the assignment of factual status are seen as stipulations of the magnitude of difference which the investigator is willing to tolerate between what the proposition proposes and what it excludes, then it will be seen that this rule fails to provide the calculable criteria for making such assessments that are found in some other rules.

The general warranting rule of participant observation may, I think, be stated thus: a proposition will be called factual if what is reported to the investigator and what is observed by him are taken as adequate evidence for the existence what the proposition proposes. The specific grounds for such a rule are protocol statements like "observer A observed such-and-such" or "such-and-such was reported by persons one, two and three to observer A." Such a warranting rule has several problems. First, the meaning relationship between the protocol statements as propositions and the new proposition is not clear. Second, the lack of standardization of the observational set-up does not ensure that each subject will have an equal opportunity to contribute to the data. And third, because of this unequal contribution the investigator has difficulty weighting the information received from subjects in order to produce a composite statement for the group. However, many users of this participant observation rule stress that their increased access to the "ongoing flow of action" enables them to apprehend facts more directly than do interviews and questionnaires before these facts have been filtered through all sorts of "artificial" processes.

Conclusions

In every science, investigators must use various procedural rules for deciding whether propositions or statements are to be judged factual and, therefore, to be admitted to the corpus of scientific knowledge. Given the procedural rules for warranting propositions, the sociological investigator must attempt to specify what kind of difference between what a proposition proposes and what it excludes he is willing to accept as evidence for or against the factual status of his proposition. In applying each procedural rule to decide matters of fact, one should be guided by the way this comparison is conducted and by the nature of the evidence the user needs to make a decision.

In examining various procedural rules in this chapter, I have tried to indicate that their application involves a number of difficulties. First, it is not at all clear (for example, with regard to validity and reliability, measures of strength of association, or control of alternative propositions) how the investigator decides about the extent to which the procedural rules are to be employed and judged. Second, the use of "existing" propositions cannot be precisely stated. From the perspective of my discussion, an "empirical" generalization is a proposition which an investigator cites to accredit his own proposition—thus warranting it as factual; "theoretical" generalizations are those propositions which do not have such a status assigned to them but which the investigator finds useful because they may be combined with other propositions to yield still other propositions whose factual status can be assigned. Third, it is unclear how the investigator fits the various pieces (the different procedural rules) together in order to make a determination about a proposition. In fact, though Zetterberg states that these rules have to be weighted into a composite judgment of acceptance or rejection, he does not tell us how to do this. That investigators frequently accomplish this judgment is not in doubt, but they do so without any standardized and communicable procedural rule.[5]

We should remember that sociological research is behavior: it is action which is covered and guided by rules. In teaching people the proper ways of doing sociology we expose them to the rules which, if successfully followed, will lead to the kinds of outcomes

[5] It is true, of course, that I have not followed any publicly available rules in my own choice of Zetterberg, Becker, and other sociologists as objects of attention here. This lack might be considered a criticism of my position but, from my viewpoint, it fully supports the arguments I advance in this chapter.

which sociologists define as normatively adequate. With this in mind, we might conceive of a hypothetical sociologist following each of the rules that I have presented in this paper. Such a puppet sociologist who acted obediently in terms of these rules in conducting research would—with the exception of the rule of statistical inference—in most cases be unable to decide issues of factuality in a methodical way. At the point of deciding the factual status of a proposition, such a puppet would "break down," would be unable to proceed any further on the basis of these preprogramed normative prescriptions. At such junctures, the sociologist would have to consult *his* common-sense knowledge of his discipline and would decide for this or that option on the basis of some lay theory.

In concluding, I wish to state again any central point: despite the fact that much of his research is extensively covered by rules, the issue of deciding factuality is only resolved through the sociologist's appeal to common-sense theories. Whether this is good or bad is not the point; it is just the way things are and should be acknowledged by the sociological community. Failure to appreciate the common-sense character of factual decisions results in ignoring the judgmental and theoretic component of such decisions. Consider, in this light, Stinchcombe's comment (1966, p. 72) on the evaluation of functional theories of stratification: "Deciding whether they are true or false is not a theoretical or ideological matter, but an empirical one." Alas, if only the world were so neatly divisible into "theoretic" and "empirical" realms, we might be able to determine factuality by merely inspecting the world. Since this is not the case and since our factual judgments are socially controlled and governed, the very act of such an inspection becomes a theoretic act in the strongest sense.

★★★★★★★★★★★★★★★★★★★

7

Paradigms and Falsification

★★★★★★★★★★★★★★★★★★★

In 1962 Thomas Kuhn published his influential *The Structure of Scientific Revolutions,* a book which has caused widespread debate and controversy among philosophers, historians of science, and scientists in a whole host of disciplines, culminating in a series of papers concerned with Kuhn's ideas in relation to those of Karl Popper. This collection of papers (Lakatos and Musgrave, 1970) includes two essays by Kuhn himself, updating his earlier views. In addition, Kuhn (1970a) has provided a "Postscript" for a new edition of his book. My intentions here are to discuss some of Kuhn's ideas as they are presented in the first edition of his book and his more recent writings; to consider these ideas in relation to those of some other writers on the history and the philosophy of science, especially Popper and his notion of falsification; and, finally, to briefly consider the relevance of these issues for sociology and sociological research.

Early Kuhn

In the original edition of his book Kuhn (1962, p. 10) argues that "particular coherent traditions of scientific research," which he refers to as "normal science," take their shape from paradigms. Although he uses the notion of paradigms in a great variety of ways, in the "Preface" (p. x) he defines them "as universally recognized scientific achievements that for a time provide model problems and solutions to a community of practitioners." These paradigms include "law, theory, applications, and instrumentation together" (p. 10) and "they are the source of the methods, problem-field, and standards of solution accepted by any mature scientific community at any given time. As a result, the reception of a new paradigm often necessitates a redefinition of the corresponding science" (p. 102). Paradigms also prepare students for the scientific community: "The study of paradigms . . . is what mainly prepares the student for membership in the particular scientific community with which he will later practice. . . . Men whose research is based on shared paradigms are committed to the same rules and standards for scientific practice. That commitment and the apparent consensus it produces are prerequisites for normal science, i.e., for the genesis and continuation of a particular research tradition" (pp. 10–11). Kuhn uses the notion of a paradigm, then, to indicate the existence of a coherent, unified viewpoint, a kind of *Weltanschauung,* which determines the way a science's practitioners view the world and practice their craft.

The other notion central to Kuhn is "normal science," which "means research firmly based upon one or more past scientific achievements, achievements that some particular scientific community acknowledges for a time as supplying the foundation for its further practice. Today such achievements are recounted, though seldom in their original form, by science textbooks, elementary and advanced" (p. 110). Normal science is practiced within the dominant paradigm. The promise of a paradigm is "achieved by extending the knowledge of those facts that the paradigm displays as particularly revealing, by increasing the extent of the match between those facts and the paradigm's predictions, and by further articulation of the paradigm itself" (p. 24). He notes that much of the effort in a mature science is in the nature of mop-up work and states that "mopping-up operations are what engage most scientists throughout their careers. They constitute what I am here calling normal science" (p. 124). The main activity of normal science, states Kuhn, is puzzle-solving, a puzzle being both restricted by rules and assured of a solution. Sometimes, of course, changes or discoveries do occur in scientific disciplines. He notes that "discovery commences with the awareness of anomaly, i.e., with the recognition that nature has somehow violated the paradigm-induced expectations that govern normal science" (pp. 52–53). That is, a persistant failure of the puzzles of normal science to come out as they should may lead to anomaly. From Kuhn's standpoint, anomaly can occur only with respect to what is expected from the worldview of those practicing within one or another paradigm: "Anomaly appears only against the background provided by the paradigm. The more precise and far-reaching that paradigm is, the more sensitive an indicator it provides of anomaly and hence of an occasion for paradigm change" (p. 65). Scientific revolutions, according to Kuhn, take place when, "confronted with anomaly or with crisis, scientists take a different attitude toward existing paradigms, and the nature of their research changes accordingly. The proliferation of competing articulations, the willingness to try anything, the expression of explicit discontent, the recourse to philosophy and to debate over fundamentals, all these are symptoms of transition from normal to revolutionary research" (p. 90).

Kuhn's views are, among other things, sharply different from those dominant in formulations of science which differentiate facts from interpretations. He questions the assumption that the world we know is a collection of individual observable "facts" which science tries to order so as to predict certain events on the basis of others. Kuhn argues that what is seen as a "problem," a "fact," a "solution," and so on depends on presuppositions which constitute part of a paradigm. These presuppositions may be metaphysical, theoretical, or otherwise and may be recognized or totally implicit.

These views of course, raise questions about the so-called cumulative nature of science, according to which science progresses by gathering new facts to construct wider, more inclusive theories.

In discussing Kuhn it is important to consider the two major points on which he has been criticized. First of all, the whole notion of a paradigm is rather unclear. Kuhn himself acknowledges this and attempts in his more recent essays to clarify his usage of the term. The lack of clarity and precision in his original edition has been shown by Masterman, who, in a rather careful attempt to elucidate Kuhn's notion of paradigm, conclude that Kuhn uses *paradigm* in at least twenty-one different senses in his original work. Not all these usages are inconsistent with one another, however, and Masterman suggests that the various senses of paradigm fall into three main groups (1970, p. 65): "metaphysical paradigms," or "metaparadigms," which concern such things as beliefs, myths, new ways of seeing, and other aspects of "a metaphysical notion or entity"; "sociological paradigms," which refer to concrete scientific achievements, universally recognized scientific achievements, and the like; and "artefact paradigms" or "construct paradigms," such as an actual textbook or classic work and other concrete manifestations. Kuhn, in responding to this criticism in the recent Lakatos and Musgrave volume (1970), tries to drop the paradigm concept altogether, substituting the term "disciplinary matrix," which he says includes symbolic generalizations, shared commitments to certain beliefs, shared values, and exemplars ("concrete problem-solutions"). All these attempts to clarify the term *paradigm* are useful. Yet, for the purposes of much of my interests here, I wish to endorse Kuhn's insistence that a paradigm in one or another science cannot be completely expressed.

The second major objection to Kuhn's views, as expressed in the first edition of his book, concerns the relativism to which it seems to lead. By stressing the determinative influence of paradigms as they affect the ways scientists view the world, including their conception of what is or is not a fact, Kuhn apparently denies the possibility of comparing and making judgments about the choice of paradigms. That is, since there are no such things as "independent" facts, or any other independent factors or standards, there can be no "good reasons" for choosing one paradigm over another.

The notion of what constitutes a good reason is paradigm-dependent. Kuhn states, for instance, that "the competition between paradigms is not the sort of battle that can be resolved by proofs" (p. 147) and adds that "in these matters neither proof nor error is at issue" (p. 150). Furthermore, "we may . . . have to relinquish the notion, explicit or implicit, that changes of paradigm carry scientists closer to the truth" (p. 119). Since how scientists define the world depends on the paradigm in which they operate, comparison of paradigms is impossible: "The normal-scientific revolution is not only incompatible but often actually incommensurable with what has gone before." What Kuhn's early arguments seem to lead to, then, is the abandonment of the idea of objectivity and progress in science.

Falsification

The view that scientific knowledge can never be "proven" knowledge is recognized by most scientists and philosophers, and a number of different positions have been taken on this recognition (such as those of Carnap and the logical positivists, and what have been termed the more "sociological" views of Polanyi and Kuhn). Perhaps the most widely accepted position today is that of Karl Popper, who says that the scientist should not devote his attention to proving the correctness of his position but rather must try to specify the conditions under which he would be willing to give up or change his position. Popper (1961) argues with his notion of "falsifiability" that no theory can ever be proven "true" with finality but that it can be proven "false" with finality. What cannot in principle be overthrown is unworthy of being seriously considered. Kuhn, in the first edition of his book, expresses skepticism over the existence of falsifying experiences: "No process yet disclosed by the historical study of scientific development at all resembles the methodological stereotypes of falsification by direct comparison with nature" (1962, p. 77). And he goes on to state: "If any and every failure to fit were ground for theory rejection, all theories ought to be rejected at all times" (p. 146).

Because Kuhn's book cast grave doubts on the possibility of Popper's notion of falsification, it is important to take a closer look at this notion. In its most crude form, Popper's view is that no scientific hypothesis can be regarded as established so long as the scientist knows only the evidence that confirms it and has not undertaken to discover evidence that disproves it. In other words, statements are to be regarded as empirically founded only when the empirical methods by which they might be disproved are specified. In Popper's words (1963, p. 38), "*Criteria for refutation* have to be laid down beforehand: it must be agreed which observable situations, if actually observed, mean that the theory is refuted." The problem which concerned Popper was to find some way of choosing among the proliferation of theories in all scientific disciplines.

While there are various types of falsification, that which is termed "sophisticated falsification" (Lakatos, 1970) best expresses the view of modern falsificationists, who are concerned not with the appraisal of a single "theory" but rather with a "series of theories." This view is summarized by Lakatos (p. 119) as follows: "no experiment, experimental report, observational statement or well-corroborated low-level falsifying hypothesis alone can lead to falsification. There is no falsification before the emergence of a better theory" (italics removed from original). And the crucial element in a "better theory" is whether it "offers any novel, excess information compared with its predecessor and whether some of the excess information is corroborated" (p. 120). Lakatos regards sophisticated falsification as stronger than Popper's ("naive") falsification, in that Popper sees falsification without requiring the necessary involvement of a better theory.

Lakatos argues that while Kuhn has perhaps been successful in casting strong doubts on the idea of naive falsification, the sophisticated brand of falsification which he advocates is not subject to the same attack. Let us first, then, look again at the early Kuhn and then at his later views with regard to (naive) falsification. Following this, I will examine Lakatos' version of falsification in light of Kuhn's views.

Later Kuhn

In the original edition of his book, Kuhn argued that paradigms function to set "puzzles" and, at the same time, to set forth the standards for their solution. From that point of view, to satisfactorily explain something is dependent on the whole scientific community's understanding of what it means to have a "satisfactory explanation." That is, the "facts" to be explained and the very notion of "explanation" itself are paradigm-dependent. He recognized, however, that "paradigm shifts" occur in all sciences but argued that these shifts could not be due to falsification, because the "facts" against which theories might be falsified were also paradigm-dependent. Rather, "anomalies" arise which, after the failure of repeated efforts to resolve them, give birth to scientific revolutions. And when scientists do repudiate an old paradigm and embrace a new one, they undergo (1962, p. 150) a "conversion experience," for "a decision of that kind can only be made on faith" (p. 157).

In the postscript to the new edition to his book and in his two essays in *Criticism and the Growth of Knowledge* (Lakatos and Musgrave, 1970), however, Kuhn appears to have changed his original position. At the very least, he has made it extremely difficult for us to know exactly what position he now holds. For one thing he now speaks of two different senses of the concept of paradigm (1970b, p. 73): On the one hand, it stands for the entire constellation of beliefs, values, techniques, and so on shared by the members of a given community. On the other, it denotes one sort of element in that constellation, the concrete puzzle-solutions which, employed as models or examples, can replace explicit rules as a basis for the solution of the remaining puzzles of normal science." Despite his attempt to clarify the notion of paradigm and to speak of its various components, Kuhn is still (necessarily, I believe) vague as to its precise meaning. But whereas he originally seemed to hold the view that there existed a kind of disciplinary *Zeitgeist* which determined the way its practitioners viewed the world and, consequently, made the comparison of paradigms impossible (paradigm incommensurability), he now speaks of the comparison of paradigms and of cross-paradigm communication.

Related to this change is Kuhn's retreat from his original position on relativism. On the one hand, he states that "if two men disagree, for example, about the relative fruitfulness of their theories, or if they agree about that but disagree about the relative importance of fruitfulness and, say, scope in reaching a choice, neither can be convicted of a mistake. Nor is either being unscientific"

(1970a, pp. 199–200). On the other hand, he asserts that there are good reasons for choosing one theory rather than another. These good reasons are "of exactly the kind standard in philosophy of science: accuracy, scope, simplicity, fruitfulness, and the like" (1970b, p. 261). Given his earlier views, one would expect that such reasons would be regarded as paradigm-dependent. Our confusion is heightened by such statements as the following: "What I am denying then is neither the existence of good reasons nor that these reasons are of the sort usually described. I am, however, insisting that such reasons constitute values to be used in making choices rather than rules of choice. Scientists who share them may nevertheless make different choices in the same concrete situation" (1970b, p. 262). (One might, of course, ask about the notion of "the same concrete situation.")

Kuhn's views are similarly ambiguous with regard to other aspects of his argument. He states (1970b, p. 267), for instance, that "though most of the same signs are used before and after a [scientific] revolution—e.g., force, mass, element, compound, cell—the way in which some of them attach to nature has somehow changed. Successive theories are thus, we say, incommensurable." Consistent with this statement is the assertion that "people do not see stimuli: our knowledge of them is highly theoretical and abstract" (1970a, p. 192). But later in the same essay he asserts (p. 201) that "the stimuli that impinge on [scientists with different paradigms] are the same." And speaking of communication breakdowns, he says (1970a, p. 276) they "are likely evidence that the men involved are processing certain stimuli differently, receiving different data from them, seeing different things or the same thing differently." In summary, then, Kuhn's views on relativism are not at all clear. While Kuhn can be faulted on his lack of clarity and his inconsistency, he has nevertheless been enormously important in sensitizing scientists to the inadequacies of the positivistic empiricism that has dominated the scientific enterprise for at least two generations.

We are still left with the question with which Kuhn began. Are there good objective reasons for scientists' proceeding as they do, or do we merely term them "good" because they are endorsed by the members of a certain scientific community? Although Kuhn's views seem mixed, the force of argument in all his writings is toward the latter alternative. I share Kuhn's views of the importance of the scientific community, as is obvious from my concern with procedural rules in the previous chapter. Before considering the importance of the scientific community further, however, I want to return to Lakatos' arguments concerning sophisticated falsification and examine them in light of some of Kuhn's, and my own, views.

Sophisticated Falsification

It will be recalled that, according to Lakatos (1970, p. 116), "for the sophisticated falsificationist a theory is 'acceptable' or 'scientific' only if it has corroborated excess empirical content over its predecessor (rival), that is, only if it leads to the discovery of novel facts." But how is this to be determined? He tells us (pp. 106–108) that the sophisticated falsificationist

makes unfalsifiable by fiat *some (spatio-temporally) singular statements which are distinguishable by the fact that there exists at the time a "relevant technique" such that "anyone who has learned it" will be able to* decide *that the statement is "acceptable." . . . This decision is then followed by a second kind of decision concerning the separation of the set of* accepted *basic statements from the rest. . . . The methodological falsificationist realizes that in the "experimental techniques" of the scientist fallible theories are involved, "in the light of which" he interprets the facts. In spite of this he "applies" these theories, he regards them in the given context not as theories under test but as* unproblematic background knowledge *"which we accept (tentatively) as unproblematic while we are testing the theory." . . . Furthermore, probabalistic theories may qualify now as "scientific": although they are not falsifiable they can be easily made "falsifiable" by an* additional (third type) decision *which the scientist can make by specifying certain rejection rules which may make statistically interpreted evidence "inconsistent" with the probabalistic theory.*

In addition, Lakatos stresses the importance of appraising a series of theories rather than isolated theories and says that such theories have to be judged in the "long run." A series of theories is "theoretically progressive" if each new theory "has some excess empirical content over its predecessor, that is, if it predicts some novel, hitherto unexpected fact" (p. 118). Such a series can also be regarded as "empirically progressive" if "some of this excess empirical content is also corroborated, that is, if each new theory leads us to the actual discovery of some *new* fact." He then adds (Lakatos, 1970: 118): "Finally, let us call a problemshift *progressive* if it is both theoretically and empirically progressive, and *degenerating* if it is not. We 'accept' problemshifts as 'scientific' only if they are at least theoretically progressive; if they are not, we 'reject' them as 'pseudoscientific.' "

The problem with all of what Lakatos says, of course, is that numerous *decisions* are involved in this falsification procedure. Kuhn, in responding to Lakatos, is sensitive to this, noting (1970b, pp. 238–239) that scientists must decide which statements to "make unfalsifiable by fiat," they must decide on a probability threshold below which statistical evidence will be held "inconsistent" with that theory, and, since research programs ("problemshifts") are to be evaluated over time, scientists must decide whether a given program at a given time is "progressive" (and "scientific") or "degenerating" (and "pseudoscientific"). What Kuhn does not point out, however, is that scientists must also decide what to regard as relevant techniques for deciding what is acceptable, they must decide what to regard as the facts as well as what to consider as new facts, they must decide what to regard as excess empirical content, they must decide what constitutes corroboration, and they must decide what length shall be considered the "long run" in determining whether a research program is to be considered progressive or degenerating. I do not mean that such decisions are made at the whim of the individual scientist, but rather that he must rely on common-sense understandings that he and his colleagues assume are taken for granted by all competent members of the particular scientific community to which he belongs. Lakatos totally ignores this whole issue.

Feyerabend (1970, p. 215) is critical of Lakatos' sophisticated falsification position because "the standards which Lakatos wants to defend are either *vacuous*—one does not know when to apply them—or they can be *criticized* on grounds very similar to those which led to them in the first place." What both Kuhn and Feyerabend emphasize in their remarks about Kuhn's decision-imperatives is the point that has been central to Kuhn's writings: decision-imperatives constitute shared ideological commitments among scientists within a given paradigm.

Whatever the lack of clarity in Kuhn's work, and despite the fact that he and Feyerabend disagree in certain respects, both writers raise important questions about the rational character of science. Popper and Lakatos, however, continue to insist that it is possible to make judgments as to which of two (or more) theories is "closer to the truth," even if the theories are from radically different paradigms. Thus, Lakatos (1970, pp. 179–180) asserts that "the growth of science takes place essentially in the world of ideas, in Plato's and Popper's 'third world,' in the world of articulated knowledge which is independent of knowing subjects" [italics deleted]. This third world is distinguished by Popper (1968a, 1968b) from two other worlds: the first world is the material world, the second world is the world of consciousness, and the third world is the world of truth and standards. According to Popper and Lakatos, the growth of knowledge takes place in this third world, where rational judgments of science are possible. Unfortunately, however, scientists live and work within the first and second worlds—the world of matter and thought.

Relevance for Sociology

There are those who argue that the social sciences are in a preparadigm stage of development. Regan (1967, p. 1385), for example, states: "We social scientists are in what Kuhn might call a 'pre-paradigm' stage of development in which consensus has yet to emerge on basic concepts and theoretical assumptions," and for Truman (1965, p. 873) the lack of a paradigm constitutes *the* problem for political science: "Redefinition and redirection will depend upon the emergence of a new and broadly based consensus about the discipline."

But is it correct to speak of a preparadigm stage in any scientific discipline? Kuhn himself is very unclear about this question. In the original edition of his book he states that "acquisition of a paradigm and of the more esoteric type of research it permits is a sign of maturity in the development of any given scientific field" (1962, p. 11). From that statement we could assume that a scientific field might function without a paradigm. Further, he says that the social sciences may be in a preparadigm stage, while the physical sciences have relatively well-developed paradigms (pp. 10–15). But in the second edition of his book he asserts that "a paradigm is what the members of a scientific community share, and conversely, a scientific community consists of men who share a paradigm" (1970a, p. 176). This latter statement indicates that a paradigm exists by virtue of the existence of a scientific community and that, therefore, paradigms are to be found in the social sciences.

But even if there were a preparadigm stage in a scientific field, is sociology located at that stage? Here, too, Kuhn's argument would seem to indicate that sociology is not at a preparadigm stage. He states that "in the sciences . . . the formation of specialized journals, the foundation of specialists' societies, and the claim for a special place in the curriculum have usually been associated with a group's first reception of a single paradigm" (1962, p. 19). Certainly, we find in sociology the existence of these three characteristics. Therefore, it seems to me incorrect to talk about the development or acquisition of paradigms in the social sciences. Kuhn himself seems to recognize this when he states that "what changes with the transition to maturity is not the presence of a paradigm but rather its nature" (1970a, p. 179).

With regard to falsification, it is in most instances difficult to imagine what would constitute falsification of a sociological "hypothesis," let alone of a theory. As an example, consider an imaginary theory about the relationship between people's positions in the social-class hierarchy and their mental health status. The sociologist conducts research to test a hypothesis involving this relationship and finds that none exists. Does he accept this lack of relationship as disproving his theory? He may or he may not. He may argue that his measures of the relevant variables need to be improved. Having done so (and having obtained another research grant), he sets out again to test his hypothesis. Again, the hypothesize relationship fails to materialize. Does he now abandon his theory? Not necessarily. He may suggest that there is some "confounding" variable that hides the relationship, and so he advances an auxiliary hypothesis.

Once again, he obtains the necessary funds, conducts his study, and finds support neither for his initial hypothesis nor for his auxiliary hypothesis. Is his theory refuted at last? Perhaps. If he is sufficiently ingenious, he may continue to propose auxiliary hypotheses and argue that his unsatisfactory results must be due to this or that or . . . , for he "knows" that his theory is correct.

Why, then, does he finally abandon his theory concerning the relationship between social class and mental illness, or any other relationship or sociological theory? Not because he and the sociological community regard it as falsified, but rather because he loses interest, is discouraged and frustrated, finds no one else particularly interested in it, cannot obtain funds to continue his research in that direction, or becomes interested in something else. There have always been plenty of what sociologists regard as theories. And there have always been plenty of candidates for truth in sociology. When old truths are replaced by new ones, it is not because of falsification but largely because, as Planck (1949) suggests, the defenders of the old truths die out.

While the idea of falsification has little direct application to the field of sociology, the issues raised by Kuhn and Popper are highly relevant to the practice of our discipline. As I noted in the previous chapter, the structure of a science can be defined in terms of the rules of procedure which determine which propositions come to be accepted as the corpus of science at a given time. It is not inconsistent with this view to accept Polanyi's assertion (1958, p. 171) that "science is a system of beliefs to which we are committed. Such a system cannot be accounted for either from experience as seen from within a different system, or by reason without any experience." For both the emphasis on procedural rules and on beliefs constitute elements of Kuhn's notion of paradigm, which (1970a, p. 175) "stands for the entire constellation of beliefs, values, techniques, and so on shared by the members of a given (scientific) community."

A Sociological View of Science

By now it is recognized in all sciences that knowledge is not the simple affair it was once taken to be. No longer are "coherence" or "correspondence" theories of truth accepted without question.

Nor are demonstrations of truth accepted solely on the basis of their logical validity, and not even when theories or hypotheses are subjected to observation are they readily accepted as the truth. Consider, for example, the problems connected with the observation of facts. What is or is not a fact? Not everyone agrees that it is something "out there" that can be observed by the objective scientist with his "rational" methods. Rather what constitutes a fact can be seen as dependent on the criteria taken for granted in one or another scientific community. Whitehead (1933, p. 284) recognized this when he remarked: "A great deal of confused philosophical thought had its origin in obliviousness to the fact that the relevance of factual evidence is dictated by theory. For you cannot test a theory by evidence which that theory dismisses as irrelevant." Whitehead seemed to have in mind what we might term "explicit theories." But whether or not something is regarded as a fact (as well as whether something is regarded as "something") is determined by different sets of presuppositions. That is, there is no such thing as "pure experience," no such thing as "facts" that are recorded directly "from nature." Theoretical presuppositions are always involved.

Even though Lakatos and Popper write of a "third world" (the world of truth and objective knowledge), the world revealed (or constructed) by scientific theories cannot exist apart from the human mind. To assert, as these writers do, that anything exists apart from thought is meaningless. Thus, there can be no scientific knowledge free of presuppositions, and it is therefore impossible to get to the bottom in any verification process. When we speak about the "facts" we are speaking about what people in a given social milieu at a given time accept as facts. If this milieu happens to be considered a scientific community, then we can speak of "scientific facts."

Unfortunately, sociology has usually ignored these issues. The influence of Durkheim, with his emphasis that "social facts are to be treated as things," has long dominated the field. His assertion (1938, p. 94), for example, that "when we come into contact with social phenomena, one is . . . surprised by the astonishing regularity with which they occur under the same circumstances" expresses the belief that phenomena exist in their own right "out there" and that their regularity exists to be discovered by the sociological investigator. The same view can be found in most sociological writings. In Riley's widely used methodology textbook (1963, p. 29), the following quotation by Conant is cited with approval: "Scientists collect their facts by observing what is happening. They group them and try to interpret them in the light of other facts that are already known." And in a recent volume sponsored by the National Academy of Sciences and the Social Science Research Council, we find this statement: "The specialist in empirical research looks toward the facts, and proceeds to locate, measure, and record data; to assure the reliability and relevance of the data; and to control other possible variables by experimental, statistical, or other techniques" (Smelser and Davis, 1969, pp. 33–34).

Although a few sociologists such as Blumer emphasize the ever-changing nature of social reality, the majority apparently believes that social reality is basically fixed and stable. One reason for this belief, especially in the United States, is the general lack of interest in and hostility toward philosophy, including the philosophy of science. Most sociologists, especially those engaged in empirical research, appear to be ignorant of the possible influence of their implicit theories on their work. In my view, presuppositions and metaphysics cannot be avoided, for as Burtt (1954, p. 229) asks: "If you cannot avoid metaphysics, what kind of metaphysics are you likely to cherish when you sturdily oppose yourself to be free from the abomination?" Consider, for instance, two of the most widespread presuppositions in all scientific inquiry: first, that there exists an Order of Things and, in particular, an Order of Nature; second, that this intelligible order in the universe can be grasped, understood, or discovered by man. It would seem that these two presuppositions are taken by most scientists as beyond doubt, not subject to revision. The relevance of presuppositions for Kuhn's paradigm notion is recognized by Toulmin (1970a, p. 40): "The *intellectual* function of Kuhn's 'paradigm' is precisely that of Collingwood's 'absolute presuppositions.' " But to speak of the intellectual "function" of paradigms in this connection is misleading, for "absolute" (and "relative" as well) presuppositions help constitute paradigms.

The two absolutes mentioned above, along with a third—that every event has a definite cause—are basic to paradigms in all scientific communities. Although the physical and social sciences share these presuppositions, they undoubtedly differ in the extent of agreement about other elements which help constitute paradigms. Kuhn points out that paradigms provide scientists with a kind of map and some directions for map-making (1962, p. 108): "In learning a paradigm the scientist acquires theory, methods, and standards together, usually in an inextricable mixture." The degree of consensus about these directions for map-making is considerably less in the social sciences than in the physical sciences (Lodahl and Gordon, 1972), but these differences do not deny that paradigms exist in the various disciplines or that in every field the scientist must acquire the paradigm through a socialization process by which he becomes a member of his scientific community.

I noted in the previous chapter that every discipline's practitioners must agree on the criteria which, for that group and that time, determine what is to be regarded as factual and as constituting knowledge. In science, then, truth cannot be regarded as conformity with the "real" but rather as conformity with standards held in a scientific community. Whereas truth is classically defined as a certain relation between propositions and reality, it is now widely accepted that meeting standards or criteria constitutes the definition of truth. Thus the entire problem involved in ascertaining fact (or truth) involves the user's rules of procedure. Of course, the language that scientists use is often misleading in this regard. We speak, for instance, of current running through a wire, even though we do not actually observe the flow. All we can observe are such phenomena as movements of the needle of a galvanometer or an ammeter. Nor do we see electrons; we have only their tracks or bubbles of vapor in a cloud chamber.

This point of view is far different from that held by many writers concerned with science. The nineteenth-century mathematician C. S. Peirce (1957, pp. 53–54) declared that "different minds may set out with the most antagonistic views, but the progress of investigation carries them by a force outside of themselves to one and the same conclusion. This activity of thought by which we are carried, not where we wish, but to a foreordained goal, is like the operation of destiny." More recently, Braithwaite (1953, pp. 367–368) states: "Man proposes a system of hypotheses: Nature disposes of its truth or falsity. Man invents a scientific system, and then discovers whether or not it accords with observed fact." Lakatos (1970, p. 130) says, "It is not that we propose a theory and nature may shout NO; rather, we propose a maze of theories, and Nature may shout INCONSISTENT." And Weyl remarks, "I wish to record my unbounded admiration for the work of the experimenter in his struggle to wrest interpretable facts from an unyielding Nature who knows so well how to meet our theories with a decisive No—or with an inaudible yes." Popper, who cites this quotation from Weyl, indicates his full agreement with it. All of these writers, then, compare theories as representations of Nature, as statements about what is "really out there."

Despite the ambiguities in his position, Kuhn declares his disagreement with such views, emphasizing that what we choose to regard as knowledge is related to the time and culture within which such decisions are made. Kolakowski (1972, p. 235), speaking of positivism, makes the same point: "The fact that contemporary positivism is unable to grasp its own relativity and dependence on specific cultural values is perhaps of no special importance: after all, the same is true of all ideologies, which assume that their own values are absolute in contradistinction to all others, and by the very same token present the acceptance of these values as a result of purely intellectual labour, devoid of ideological considerations." This point should be fully grasped: it is not that positivism or some other "ism" is ideological while another is not, nor that paradigms are found in some sciences and not in others, nor even that paradigms exist in scientific communities but not elsewhere. Rather, all human communities are *language* communities, and in learning a language we learn how to look at (what we call) the world. That is, thinking can occur only within a linguistic framework that is social. In Hampshire's words: "We cannot step outside the language which we use, and judge it from some ulterior and superior vantage point" (1956, p. 192). This view is, of course, contrary to those which appeal to extralinguistic reference.

Kuhn begins to grasp this point in the final essay in *Criticism and the Growth of Knowledge,* but only partially. He states (1970b, p. 270), "In learning a science or a language, vocabulary is generally acquired together with at least a minimal battery of generalizations which exhibit it applied to nature." Whereas I think he is correct in one way, he insists on separating science and language when he refers to science "or" language, as if science could be learned in some manner other than through language.

Kuhn's arguments concerning language could be strengthened by giving it explicit attention. He does hint at this the importance of language in the Postscript (1970a, p. 205): "The proponents of different theories are like the members of different language-culture communities," although he does not pursue it. Still, Kuhn is far more sensitive to language than are most philosophers and historians of science and most social scientists, who generally seem unwilling to recognize that language cuts up the world in different ways. Sociologists, especially, fail to realize that what words mean is determined by the form of life in which they belong. In sociology, as in all scientific disciplines, the scientific community is defined partially by its accepted presuppositions, which then function to prescribe the rules that determine what are to be regarded as scientific problems, as acceptable research, and as solutions to these problems. These "rules" include not only formal procedural rules but the common-sense theories and methods that the sociologist must consult and utilize when faced with numerous choices and decisions in his inquiries. In all sciences, practitioners are constantly forced to make decisions about what to consider as relevant factors in testing a *ceteris paribus* clause, what to regard as stimuli, what to consider inconsistent findings, what constitutes similarity, and so on.

The more formal (procedural) rules are learned when the scientist is socialized into his discipline. The members of a given scientific community can be regarded, in Kuhn's (1970b, p. 253) words, as "men bound together by common elements in their education and apprenticeship, aware of each other's work, and characterized by relative fullness of their professional communication and the relative unanimity of their professional judgment." All of this involves language and, therefore, places a broad parameter on what scientists do, on what they can say and, most importantly, on the kinds of things that can be thought. Thinking occurs within a linguistic framework that is social, so that whenever we use a given word in such and such a circumstance we are assuming the whole "grammar" of that word in its ordinary use and cannot avoid doing so. In short, we cannot escape language: "We cease to think if we do not do so under the constraint of language" (Nietszche, 1955, p. 862).

This dependence on language characterizes all science, but it presents a particular difficulty for the social sciences, a difficulty which Winch describes at length in *The Idea of a Social Science* (1953). While all scientists must acquire the rules of a given scientific community, the social scientist must also be socialized to the rules of the people whom he studies. The study of anything at all is a human activity, but a physicist studying an electron, for example, need not be concerned that the electron may characterize its own behavior in some way or another different from his characterization, for the electron holds no theory about itself. In contrast, the "phenomena" of interest to the sociologist have ideas, beliefs, and theories about what they are doing and why.

One characteristic that distinguishes human beings from other organisms is that humans follow rules. An individual in interaction with another must have some theories or notions about how the other is likely to act, how the other will respond to his actions, and the like. In a sense, both actors must know there are rules, for all social activities are rule-ridden. Knowing there are rules is different from knowing what the rules are, for obviously people can be mistaken or ignorant concerning them, but without their existence social life would be impossible. One of the sociologist's tasks is to grasp these rules so as to understand people's motives, goals, choices, and plans. However, contrary to what most sociologists appear to believe, these are not in some way "discovered." Granted that people's reasons are regarded as having certain effects, generally on their actions, it is important to emphasize that sociological inquiry does not involve discovering these reasons or their connection with social actions. Rather, it assesses arguments: a sociological explanation considers features of the background as justifying or providing accounts for people's actions.

Max Weber, more than most sociologists, at least partially grasped this point when he emphasized the importance of "interpretive understanding," but, like most sociologists, he apparently believed that the appropriate procedure for verifying one or another interpretation was to establish statistical regularities based on the collection of empirical data. Statistical laws or regularities, however, have nothing to do with the correctness of an interpretation. If a proferred interpretation does not verify a hypothesis, statistics are not the ultimate criteria for determining its correctness, as Weber seemed to suggest. Since I pursue this line of reasoning (including the importance of justifications and accounts) in Chapter Nine, I will say no more about it at this time. The essential point here is that the sociologist must be concerned not only with the procedural rules of his discipline but with the rules which guide the behavior of those whom he studies.

Conclusions

Sociology shares many of the problems that characterize all sciences, problems that have been pointed to by such writers as Popper and Kuhn, but at the same time there are additional problems peculiar to the study of human beings. All sciences have difficulties with objectivity, although one need not accept the suggestion of some of Kuhn's critics that the idea of objectivity be completely surrendered, if one recognizes that objectivity consists in meeting a generally accepted procedural rule within a scientific (or other) community. But sociologists must also deal with the "objective" meanings of the actions and behavior of those they study. This problem need not be insurmountable so long they do not forget that the objective meaning of acoustic or visual phenomena is that meaning attributed to those signs by a rule generally accepted according to a given scheme of interpretation within a social group.

By discussing paradigms and falsification I raised questions about the whole presumption on which much contemporary sociology is based: that if only the sociologist can emulate the practice of natural and physical scientists he will achieve the success he wants. The dominant view in sociology represents a commitment to a certain definition of what it means to practice sociology. But, as I have tried to indicate, the dominant view indicates a totally unreflexive view of science and its own nature. Further, most contemporary sociology shows an irresponsibility toward, and does violence to, language. It is time we turned away from our vulgar imitations of what we mistakenly think physical scientists do and looked in other directions, perhaps to considering sociological inquiry itself as a topic for investigation. Hopefully, my discussion of paradigms and falsification will help to remind some sociologists of the need for stopping to reflect on how they deal with these problems in their work and, indeed, in their lives.

★★★★★★★★★★★★★★★★

8

Sociology as a Form of Life

★★★★★★★★★★★★★★★★

The notion of a "form of life" comes from Ludwig Wittgenstein (1954), who advanced the thesis that language and life rest entirely on social conventions. I intend in this chapter to consider sociology as a form of life, but before doing so it is useful to contrast very briefly the views of the "later" Wittgenstein with those he expressed in his earlier writings. In the *Tractatus* (1922) Wittgenstein argued that language is a picture of reality and that the general framework of any factual language is fixed objectively in advance. Since the structure of reality determines the structure of language, there should be a similarity between that which pictures and that which is pictured. The form of language, then, must be identical to that of reality. Language, Wittgenstein believed at that time, disguises thought. The only way the real forms of thought can become apparent is to break down language into its ultimate components—elementary propositions. And whether an elementary proposition is true or false can only be determined by comparing it with reality. Wittgenstein believed that logical form is also the form of reality. Thus, the concept of logical form is assumed to belong to ontology as well as to logic. In a very general way, Wittgenstein's views as expressed in the *Tractatus* can be considered as a theory of verification through sense experience: a proposition must be analyzed so as to specify under what conditions of observation it is true.

Eventually Wittgenstein came to question these views. For example, in the *Philosophical Investigations* (1958, p. 1) he notes that, according to one view of human language, "the individual words in language name objects—sentences are combinations of such means. In this picture of language we find the roots of the following idea: Every word has a meaning. This meaning is correlated with the word. It is the object for which the word stands." Wittgenstein remarks on that view of language as follows:

> *As if there were only one thing called "talking about a thing." Whereas in fact we do the most various things with our sentences. Think of exclamations alone, with their completely different functions.*
>
> *Water!*
> *Away!*
> *Ow!*
> *Help!*
> *Fine!*
> *No!*
>
> *Are you inclined still to call these words "names of objects?"* [*p. 1*].

Thus, Wittgenstein is highly critical of the picture view of language that he had advanced in the *Tractatus.* What, then, it might be asked, is a word's meaning? Wittgenstein answers, "The meaning of a word is its use in the language" (p. 43). Or, more precisely, it is its use in a particular language game. Wittgenstein (1954, p. 23) states that the term "*'language game'* is meant to bring into prominence the fact that the *speaking* of language is part of an activity, of a form of life" (p. 23). Therefore, we must consider speech as part of one or another way of life, along with eating, sleeping, and other activities. There is not, he argued, some correct usage for words that holds for all language games or for all forms of life. What we must do is look at how words are actually used in everyday situations.

From the point of view of Wittgenstein's thesis in the *Philosophical Investigations,* there can be no independent or objective sources of support outside of human thought and language. Consider the following passages from the *Investigations:*

> *And to imagine a language means to imagine a form of life.* [*p. 19*]
>
> *"So you are saying that human agreement decides what is true and what is false?"—It is what human beings* say *that is true and false; and they agree in the* language *they use. That is not agreement in opinions but in form of life.* [*p. 241*]

There is no external or objective reality against which to compare or measure a universe of discourse: "What has to be accepted, the given is—so one could say—*forms of life*" (p. 226). There are no standards existing outside of language which can be used to justify, for example, a statement's truth or falsity. The only possible justification lies in the linguistic practices which embody them: how people think and speak. The criteria for knowledge, truth, or this or that, then, do not lie outside language, nor are they a gift from God. Rather, they arise from and are only intelligible in the contexts of modes of social life. This position implies that the "social reality" which concerns sociologists does not exist independently of their methods for producing it. So it is to these methods I now turn.

In writing about sociology, one necessarily displays his own favored method of anaylsis, his way of "seeing sociologically." His writing shows his form of life as a sociologist, his version of theorizing. However, he need not always explicitly state or formulate his theory, for, as Wittgenstein emphasized, "showing" one's theory goes beyond merely talking about it. One way a sociologist shows his theorizing is by demonstrating when and where he stops doubting. With regard to their concern with social phenomena, most sociologists extend the limits of their doubt beyond the limits guiding the everyday inquiries of most laymen. And, of course, seeing sociologically is different from seeing, say, psychologically, as regards where one stops doubting. But in everyday and scientific thought alike, there are always conditions we accept without further doubt. Man could not function, men could carry on neither their everyday activities nor their scientific endeavors without some limits on their doubts. In other words, some things are always glossed; it is inevitable that not everything can be fully explicated.

In conducting his inquiries every sociologist accepts certain conditions which he cannot conceive of doubting. As I point out in the following pages, "cause" is such a condition for most sociologists. The majority simply cannot think of social phenomena without assigning cause. And while I have some rather critical remarks to make about cause and some other elements of the dominant form of life in sociology, this obviously does not mean that there are no limits to my own doubts. Specifically, I cannot imagine a social world which did not require the use of such notions as "reason" or "purpose." That is to say, doubt loses its sense for me when it comes to questions about reasons and purposes for I simply cannot conceive of most social actions as being performed without reason or purpose. To me, there is no doubt about this. My certainty is an aspect of the way I live; it is bedrock, part of my form of life, sociologically. Thus, every form of life rests on certain stipulations that can be questioned or criticized from the perspective of another form of life.

As I argue more extensively in the following chapter, all sociological analysis, including that demonstrated here, can be seen as the sociologist's method for viewing society (in this case, sociology) in one possible form. This form is, from my point of view, a possible version. It is a creation, not a concrete description. As Wittgenstein (1922, p. 342) once stated: "the fact that it can be described by Newtonian Mechanics tells us nothing about the world; but this tells us something, namely, that the world can be described in that particular way in which as a matter of fact it is described."

In this chapter, then, I am not arguing that this is the way sociology "really" is. I am not engaged in detailed description or in empirical research, in the usual sense, but rather am formulating sociology in such a way as to show a possible version of language and social life. In speaking of conflicts and contradictions in the dominant form of life of sociology, I am displaying a commitment to another election, another version of seeing sociologically, that is revealed in my analysis. Therefore, it is not my argument that the dominant version of sociology is wrong but that I do not choose to speak their language, to live sociologically in the terms they create.

As I noted in the previous chapter, sociologists have been strongly influenced by Durkheim's admonition that they deal with "social facts" as things (Durkheim, 1938, p. 1): "But in reality there is in every society a certain group of phenomena which may be differentiated from those studied by other natural sciences. When I fulfill my obligations as a brother, husband, or citizen, when I execute my contracts, I perform duties which are defined, externally to myself and my acts, in law and custom. Even if they conform to my sentiments and I feel their reality subjectively, such reality is still objective, for I did not create them; I merely inherited them through my education."

Durkheim goes on (p. 3) to note that "here, then, is a category of facts with very distinctive characteristics: it consists of ways of acting, thinking, and feeling, external to the individual, and endowed with a power of coercion, by reasons of which they control him." What Durkheim is emphasizing in his thesis concerning social facts is the existence of a social reality independent of the consciousness of individuals, something "external" to human inquirers. That is, the "facts" exist independently of the interests, motives, or whatever, of concrete individuals. Of course, Durkheim himself takes for granted and raises no questions about the nature of motives, interests, or individuals. Furthermore, he requires that we see social facts as external "forces" exercising constraints on the individual. And he requires us to accept the factuality of social phenomena as, in a sense, beyond doubt.

In telling us to focus on social facts as things, Durkheim shows a concern that our research be directed to what is "really" external (1938, p. 27): "to treat phenomena as things is to treat them as data, and these constitute the point of departure of science." We locate these things as data, Durkheim (pp. 31, 35) instructs us, through the "eradication of all preconceptions" and by finding and investigating "a group of phenomena defined in advance by certain common external characteristics." Unfortunately, he never tells us how to accomplish either of these aims. I have already discussed some of the issues connected with the eradication of preconceptions, and the identification of certain "common external characteristics" seems equally problematic. Thus, while Durkheim may serve as the authority for many contemporary sociologists who follow these admonitions, Durkheim himself presupposes the nature of his authority. It is simply taken for granted.

In considering the nature of "phenomena defined in advance by certain external characteristics," we need only recall my discussion in the last chapter of "similarity," "new facts," and the like. Awareness of this issue can be seen in the work of Garfinkel and some of the ethnomethodologists, who are explicitly concerned with such notions as "common and external." In Garfinkel's words: (1967, p. vii): "[I]n contrast to certain versions of Durkheim that teach that the objective reality of social facts is sociology's fundamental principle, the lesson is taken instead, and used as a study policy, that the objective reality of social facts *as* an ongoing accomplishment of the concerted activities of social life, with the ordinary, artful ways of that accomplishment being by members known, used, and taken for granted, is, for members doing sociology, a fundamental phenomenon."

Within the form of life shared by Durkheim and most contemporary sociologists, however, questions or problems pertaining to getting rid of preconceptions and to recognizing common external characteristics are treated as if they did not exist or had been successfully resolved. Like Durkheim, most sociologists are concerned with getting on with their investigations into these social facts, and they accept without question his version of the "appropriate" manner for acquiring knowledge. My point is not that Durkheim has failed to explicate the authority for his knowledge while others have been explicit, but rather that these taken-for-granted aspects of sociological inquiry are seldom taken as a topic for sociological consideration.

Along with a conception of social facts as external forces which operate as social constraints—forces which are considered to be the appropriate focus of sociological inquiry—goes a concern with discovering these external social facts. As did Durkheim, most sociologists hold the view that there exists a social reality independent of language and social actors, to be discovered by the application of the proper rules of sociological procedure. Thus, Labovitz and Hagedorn (1971, p. 11) state that "to achieve the major goal of science, which is to establish causal laws, facts and relations between variables must be established. The criteria to establish facts and relations are the procedures of the scientific method." And Smelser (1969, p. 13) speaks of "sociological explanation" as "that enterprise of accounting for regularities, variations, and interdependencies among the phenomena identified with the sociological framework." He notes elsewhere, where he attempts to compare and contrast the different social sciences with one another, that there must exist some "common language" in the social sciences (Smelser, 1968, p. 43): "The language I have employed is the language of the ingredients of science: dependent variables, independent variables, theoretical frameworks, and research methods." What Smelser fails to acknowledge is that there are fundamental disagreements in the various social sciences about the nature of this common language (for example, Winch, 1958; Taylor, 1964; Louch, 1966). At issue are such statements as Smelser's that this is "the language of the ingredients of science." Rather than reviewing the appropriateness of a specific assertion, I want to examine this view of science and its central position in sociology as a form of life.

Much sociological writing, especially in introductory textbooks, draws territorial boundaries to distinguish the approach and subject matter of sociology from that of other disciplines. Smelser, for example, spends more than forty pages comparing and contrasting sociology with economics, political science, anthropology, history, and psychology, in order to "explore the distinctive characteristics of sociology and its relations to the other social sciences." Among other things, he states that "With reference to sexual behavior and attitudes, for instance, sociological research can provide insight as to the types of class background and family structure associated with distinctive patterns of sexual behavior; psychological research can provide evidence as to how social and other variables are processed intra-psychically, thus contributing more microscopic kinds of insight; and historical and anthropological research can shed light on how these social and psychological determinants have worked out in diverse cultural contexts" (1968, pp. 41–42).

Smelser thus sets up the "division of labor" for several of the social sciences. In so doing, he treats as totally unproblematic his own knowledge which allows him to establish these territorial boundaries and this division of labor. His discussion of these boundaries offers no justification for their establishment, and he gives no account of the knowledge which allows him to decide where and how they are to be drawn. The point here is that a sociology which stipulates in a very concrete manner the territory it rules can be seen as taking for granted, and leaving unexplored, the source of its knowledge. For sociologists to say that such-and-such is or is not sociological, or, as I have often heard said, that a particular man's work is not "really" sociology, tells us nothing of the grounds for this knowledge. In a very profound sense, sociology as a form of life which concerns itself with boundaries exempts itself from scrutiny.

Consider a second aspect of the form of life depicted by sociology: its deterministic viewpoint. By concerning itself with causality and prediction, it commits itself to a deterministic view of nature. To see this, and to see some of the problems connected with such a view, let us return to Smelser's discussion of the ingredients of science and consider them one at a time. Smelser (1968, p. 5) begins by stating, "First, it is necessary to specify what aspect of the concrete subject matter preoccupies the investigator. . . . Sociologists are not interested in every aspect of the family; they focus on patterns of rights and obligations of family members, changes in the rate of family formation and dissolution, differences in fathers' and sons' career patterns, and so on. By asking such questions, we identify the distinctive *scientific problems, phenomena to be explained,* or *dependent variables* of a discipline." Now clearly, when Smelser speaks of patterns, changes, differences, and so on, all these presuppose entire bodies of knowledge. For an investigator to "see" patterns, changes, or differences presupposes some notion of these phenomena. There are numerous possible ways of "seeing" patterns, for instance, in the movements of human beings. But seeing is dependent on theory. Hanson (1958, p. 19), in *Patterns of Discovery,* discusses this point: "There is a sense, then, in which seeing is a 'theory-laden' undertaking. Observation of x is shaped by prior knowledge of x." The visitor to the physicist's laboratory, for instance, (p. 17) "must learn some physics before he can see what the physicist sees. . . . The infant and the layman can see: they are not blind. But they cannot see what the physicist sees; they are blind to what he sees."

The whole matter of what it is to see something is generally ignored by sociologists. While many do recognize that there may be more than one interpretation of the "same" data or the "same" thing, they fail to consider the enormous problems involved in observation. They assume that observers begin with, or "observe," the same data, as if it were only a matter of good eyesight or looking in the right place. But as Hanson points out, there is more to seeing than meets the eyeball. Wittgenstein's remarks (1958, p. 200) on this problem are helpful here:

> *Take as an example the aspects of a triangle. The triangle can be seen as a triangular hole, as a solid, as a geometrical drawing; as standing on its base, as hanging from its apex; as a mountain, as a wedge, as an arrow or pointer, as an overturned object which is meant to stand on the shorter side of the right angle, as a half parallelogram, and as various other things.*
> *"You can think now of* this *now of* this *as you look at it, can regard it now as* this *now as* this, *and then you will see it now* this *way, now* this." What *way?*

At issue, then, is not how we see something, but rather that there is a difference between a physical state and a visual experience. It is not a matter of different interpretations—different ways of thinking about something—but of seeing as an experiental state. Wittgenstein (1958, p. 212) says: "Do I really see something different each time, or do I only interpret what I see in a different way? I am inclined to say the former. But why? To interpret is to think, to do something; seeing is a state."

Thus two sociologists may, in a sense, "look at" the same retinal/cortical/sense-data, but they do not necessarily "see" the same thing, although part of the socialization process of every science is aimed toward learning to see in a similar way. There is, we might say, a linguistic factor in seeing. Consider, for instance,

Köhler's famous goblet-and-faces drawing, which to some people represents a goblet and, to others, two men staring at one another. Different people seeing the drawing see different things. And the same person, at different times, may see either the goblet or the two men. I look and see two men facing one another. Later I look again and see the goblet but not the two faces. The drawing has not changed. What has changed is what I "see." Some might ask: But what is it "really?" Such a question makes no sense here.

In order to see this or that (patterns, regularities, whatever) we must already have certain types of knowledge. Unless one is familiar with faces or goblets, he will see neither. Imagine that someone is familar with faces but has never seen a goblet. We ask him repeatedly: "Don't you see that goblet?" He says no, and then tells us that he does not know what a goblet is. We might tell him that a goblet is something like a glass or cup. That could help. But unless he is familiar with glasses and cups, this similarity will not help him either. This is not to say that in Köhler's drawing an individual will always see faces if he is unfamiliar with goblets. For people can be blind to what others see. Again, consider an example from Wittgenstein (1958, p. 211):

> *Someone tells me: "I looked at the flower, but was thinking of something else and was not conscious of its colour." Do I understand this?—I can imagine a significant context, say his going on: "Then I suddenly* saw *it, and realized it was the one which. . . ."*
>
> *Or again: "If I had turned away then, I could not have said what colour it was."*
>
> *"He looked at it without seeing it." There is such a thing. But what is the criterion for it?—Well, there is a variety of cases here.*
>
> *"Just now I looked at the shape rather than the colour." Do not let such phrases confuse you. Above all, don't wonder "What can be going on in the eyes or brain."*

To "see" sociologically, to see "changes" or "authoritarianism" or "families" or "careers" is not merely, then, a matter of looking. I quoted Hanson earlier as saying that the infant and the layman cannot see what the physicist sees. Nor can they see what the sociologist sees. That Smelser and other sociologists can see patterns and so on is not in question. But the extent to which they can see this or that involves their sharing knowledge and theories about this or that. Their methods for doing so are available in *their* corpus of knowledge, but they are totally unanalyzed and not made available to the reader. It is not that I or someone else who rejects the dominant positivist position, held by Smelser and most sociologists, can make my methods explicit, while they cannot. Rather it is the differences in our positions regarding science and sociology—in the languages we speak—that need to be explicated.

Smelser (1968, p. 5) continues as follows with his list of criteria: "Second, it is necessary to specify what each discipline treats as the distinctive causes (or determinants, or factors, or conditions) of variation in the dependent variables. . . . In accounting for variations in divorce rates, the sociologist turns to the society's degree of urbanization and industrialization; its levels of interreligious, interethnic, and interclass marriage; and its laws affecting divorce. In this search for associated conditions, the social scientist attempts to identify distinctive *independent variables.*" Again, such a statement presupposes a corpus of knowledge available both to Smelser and to the sociological investigator. Not only is Smelser able to tell us what we should do, but he *knows* (and assumes that the reader does as well) how to identify urbanization, industrialization, and so forth, as well as "distinctive" independent variables.

He goes on to state further (pp. 5–6):

> *The focus of a scientific discipline, then, can be specified by listing the dependent and independent variables that preoccupy its investigators. But these lists of variables do not tell the whole story. It is necessary, third, to specify the ways in which a discipline imposes a* logical ordering *on its variables. Indeed, merely by distinguishing between dependent and independent variables, we elicit one instance of logical ordering—that is, specifying which variables are to be viewed as causes and which as effects. On the basis of this ordering, various* hypotheses—*statements of the conditions under which dependent variables may be expected to vary in certain ways —can be formulated. A more complex kind of ordering results when*

> *a number of hypotheses are combined into an organized system (often called a* model). . . . *These models are embedded in a number of definitions, assumptions, and postulates. . . . Such definitions, assumptions, and postulates constitute the* theoretical framework *of a scientific discipline.*

Within this framework the specific hypotheses "make sense." As with his other criteria of science, there are a number of difficulties here. First of all, as I noted earlier, this position simply assumes the existence of "social facts" and a deterministic view of the universe. Like Mannheim's intellectuals (whom I will discuss shortly), however, sociologists apparently stand outside these deterministic influences. Second, to speak of the necessity of imposing a "logical ordering" is to ignore the matter of why we should do so and what is meant by the notion. Of course, sociologists do speak this way, but the authority for their knowledge that we should proceed in this manner is not revealed. From my viewpoint, there is no objective basis which will justify logical "ordering" or "inference." The only possible justification is that this is how people think and speak. For sociologists to speak of "causes" and "effects," then, represents a commitment to a certain way of speaking and to a particular form of life, which are unanalyzed and simply regarded as obvious.

The dominance of this "natural science method," with an emphasis on deductive forms of explanation and on causes and effects, is not peculiar to Smelser and can be seen in virtually any introductory text or methods book. For instance, Labovitz and Hagedorn (1970, p. 3) state that "cause, in one way or another, is central to the goal of establishing scientific laws. In general terms, causation refers to the factors that make designated phenomena happen or change." Sjoberg and Nett (1968, p. 27) remark: "Implicit in the application of the scientific method is the notion that some events occur prior to or concurrently with others and that the former have an impact on the latter, thereby generating, or causing specific reactions." And Blalock (1964, p. 9) notes that "the concepts of forcings and causes are obviously closely related, as are the notions of responses and effects." He then goes on to add that "if X is a cause of Y, we have in mind that a change in X produces a change in Y and not merely that a change in X is followed by or associated with a change in Y" [italics removed]. Blalock acknowledges (p. 11) that there are "some problems with causal thinking," but what he means by "problems" are such objections as the idea that new variables can always be introduced in such a way that causal laws cannot possibly be negated, that certain simplifying assumptions about other variables must be made if one is to empirically evaluate a causal relationship between two variables, that each effect cannot be assumed to have only one cause, and that we have no systematic way of knowing whether or not we have located all the relevant causal variables. These problems are procedural in a sense, having to do with locating the "right" causes.

There are, however, more substantial problems with the notion of cause as applied in the social sciences. One, which I shall consider in the following chapter, concerns the counterargument that actions are performed for reasons: desires, aims, purposes, goals, intentions, and the like. This position has been discussed at length by such writers as Louch, Winch, and Taylor—none of whom is a card-carrying sociologist. Perhaps because they are not regarded as sociologists, their views are almost totally ignored by most sociologists—especially in the United States. As I hope to show in the next chapter, they raise important questions about the dominant form of explanation in sociology.

We know that most sociologists speak of psychological, sociological, and social structural causes: authoritarianism, other-directedness, alienation, need for social approval, social class, religiosity, attitudes, values, norms, and so on. If there are, indeed, causal laws, as Smelser, Blalock, and most sociologists argue, one wonders if they themselves are subject to these laws. What caused them to argue for causal laws? What caused them to write their books? What social facts exercised external constraints on these men? Imagine that we located a regularity we wished to account for: that men employed by universities write more books than men employed elsewhere. How would Blalock, for example, account for this regularity if we were asking him why he wrote a particular book? Would he, like Durkeim, speak of "ways of acting, thinking, and feeling external to the individual, and endowed with a power of coercion, by reasons of which they control him?" I seriously doubt that he, or any other sociologist, would account for his own behavior by bringing it under a general causal law. And it seems almost totally unlikely that he would appeal to external forces that "caused" him to write this or that particular book, or to use those particular words. Rather, I suspect that Blalock, and most other sociologists, would employ an entirely different vocabulary, a different form of explanation, in accounting for why he wrote his books.

Sociologists would, I believe, employ purposive rather than mechanistic or deterministic explanations. A particular book was written for the "purpose" of conveying a certain point of view or message, or the writer "desired" to get his ideas known to others, or he "intended" to show the superiority of his ideas, or he "wanted" to become rich or famous or get a promotion, or for some other *reason*. I have certainly never heard sociologists account for their own actions—writing books, doing this or that type of research, becoming sociologists—by appeal to causal laws. This is not to say that I have never heard them account for the behavior of their fellow sociologists by citing deterministic or mechanistic explanations.

Now some will argue that I am not being serious, that I have created a kind of straw man to attack, for, they might assert, no one would be so foolish as to try to account for the writing of books by appealing to causal laws. Maybe so. But then we are being told that some things fall under causal laws and others do not. Looking at almost any introductory textbook, we find sociologists citing causal explanations for numerous social phenomena: voting behavior, occupational choices, birth rates, and so on. How, then, do sociologists decide when and where causal explanations are called for? (We might even ask what "causes" them to decide.) Never mind that causal explanations are set forth in probabalistic terms, the question still holds.

Of course, sociology as a form of life is like that: sociologists do sometimes appeal to causal explanations and other times do not. But I would expect them to be troubled by the implications of taking deterministic or mechanistic explanations of social behavior seriously in the first place. What would it mean if *all* behavior fell under causal laws and were completely determined? Unless it were held that all of our speech, everything we say, is determined by external causal forces which constrain us to say what we say, unless it were held that "everything"—every utterance, every movement—is determined by forces lying outside ourselves, deterministic causal explanations are not even conceivable. Most human speech is *intentional* behavior. Stating, deciding, or asserting such-and-such requires the intentional utterance of words. But if determinism were true, no one could *say* anything. They could not, therefore, state that determinism is true. If someone did state that "determinism is true," the very occurrence of his intentional speech act would imply that determinism is false. So long as we are willing to grant that people's speech is intentional behavior, we cannot accept determinism. For when we do, anyone's assertion that determinism is true is necessarily false.

What we could do, and what sociologists do when they speak about causal laws and the like, is regard determinism as true for others but not for ourselves. Further, most would probably respond to these remarks by saying that no sociologist holds such an "overdeterministic" viewpoint as that described. They would perhaps say that no social behavior is completely determined or caused, or that behavior has multiple causes, or that this is not what they mean by cause. But how do they know? And what do they mean when they speak about cause? How is it possible that sociologists can employ a term with such assurance without ever considering what it means and how it is used, and without considering their own knowledge which allows them to speak in such a manner?

Returning now to Smelser's discussion of the ingredients of science, one can, as Smelser does, speak of a theoretical framework as being "constituted" by definitions, assumptions, and postulates. But why should we? What bodies of knowledge are available which allow us to do so? Finally, the idea that a specific hypothesis "makes sense" within a particular theoretical framework represents a prime example of the point I have been trying to make. Given a specific theoretical framework and a particular hypothesis, what does the sociological investigator have to know to determine whether or not the hypothesis makes sense? To answer that it "fits," is "consistent with," or in a similar manner, simply glosses the issue. In what way must one look at the world, what (commonsense or other) knowledge must one have to see something as "making sense"?

Finally, we come to the last of Smelser's (1968, p. 6) criteria: "Fourth, it is necessary to specify the *means employed to accept or reject statements* in the various scientific disciplines. These include the methods of scientific inquiry—such as the experimental—as well as specific techniques and instruments for collecting, measuring, and processing data." Since I have considered the issue of methods at length in Chapter Six, it is not necessary to repeat my arguments here. Suffice it to say that the rules of procedure used in deciding if what a proposition proposes is warranted do not exhaust the decisions the sociologist must make in deciding on this or that option. Rather, the investigator must frequently appeal to what I call "commonsense" theories.

Although I have referred to commonsense theories in the past three chapters, it now occurs to me that this term may be somewhat misleading. Therefore, I will try to distinguish it from another notion which may be more appropriate in this context: "conventional wisdom." The notion of common sense as I have been using it comes from the writings of such phenomenologists as Husserl and Schutz, and it has been heavily used recently by Garfinkel and the ethnomethodologists. Schutz (in Emmet and MacIntyre, 1970, pp. 5–6, 11) uses the notion of common sense when speaking of social reality: "By the term "social reality" I wish to be understood the sum total of objects and occurrences within the social cultural world as experienced by the commonsense thinking of men living their daily lives among their fellow-men, connected with them in manifold relations of interaction. . . . In terms of commonsense thinking in everyday life men have knowledge of these various dimensions of the social world in which they live." Schutz is pointing to our taking for granted our actual and potential knowledge of the meaning of human actions and their products. But he is speaking of people in their everyday social lives and the manner in which they constitute themselves in the phenomena which their commonsense world takes for granted. His usage, therefore, refers to commonsense thinking within a particular language game and a particular form of life.

The sociologist, however, not only frequently shares the form of life of those whom he is studying (or at least certain aspects of it), but he also shares a particular form of life by virtue of his membership in the sociological community. Those commonsense elements which he shares with other sociologists are what I shall hereafter refer to as conventional wisdom, meaning that they are part of the taken-for-granted sources and content of knowledge within sociology. As an example of what I intend here, recall my discussion in Chapter Six of the control of "alternative" propositions or variables in warranting a sociological proposition. I pointed out that the investigator cannot specify the universe of possible alternatives or variables which he considered, nor how he decided to consider some and not others. But within the form of life of sociology, he knows that he can rely on the conventional wisdom shared with other sociologists in carrying out his task. Sociology's procedures, including those appealed to and utilized in an implicit manner, are themselves socially organized devices, taken for granted, but dependent upon the conventional wisdom of this form of life. From a slightly different perspective, we might regard this conventional wisdom as one of the elements of the sociological paradigm.

Another aspect of this form of life is the views and usage of language which characterize much sociological research. On the one hand, sociologists follow a mode of analysis where social behavior and actions are "explained," "accounted for," or "caused" by a whole host of social factors. Sociologists often explain differences in people's behaviors and activities by citing, for example, the "influence" of social-class position or ethnicity. Usually their empirical investigations involve asking people questions, the responses or answers to which allow the investigator to establish their social-class position, ethnicity, or whatever, as well as the differences among them in whatever it is that is to be explained. The sociologist assumes that language has the same meaning for everyone. While people are assumed to differ in myriad ways, the way they understand and employ speech behavior is generally assumed to be the same for everyone. By assuming that word connotations are uniform across groups, sociologists ignore the existence of differing linguistic communities or forms of life. Some writers, but few of them sociologists (Cicourel, 1964, is the best-known exception), have been critical of this view. Dell Hymes (1964, p. 20) points out that "the case in clear in bilingualism, we do not expect a Bengali using English as a fourth language for certain purposes of commerce to be influenced deeply in world views by its syntax." But, he goes on to add, "what is necessary is to realize that the monolingual situation is problematic as well. People do not all everywhere use language to the same degree, in the same situations, or for the same things." Even though language is, in a sense, all there is, sociologists conduct research by taking for granted, or suspending, questions concerning language. By glossing an actual practice which they might take as a topic for inquiry, they are better able to communicate with their colleagues and to solicit agreement from them that they have followed the "correct" procedure. Again, sociology refuses to treat itself as a phenomenon for investigation.

Another fundamental feature of most contemporary sociology is the ideal of objectivity, the ideal that knowledge should be acquired and confirmed in such a manner that neither the sociological investigator himself nor given situational circumstances will distort the phenomena of interest. Mannheim was one of the first to emphasize the influence of implicitly held presuppositions (1968, pp. 89–90): "The danger in presuppositions does not lie merely in the fact that they are prior to empirical knowledge. It lies rather in the fact that an ontology handed down through tradition obstructs new developments, especially in the basic modes of thinking, and as long as the particularity of the conventional theoretical framework remains unquestioned, we will remain in the toils of a static mode of thought. . . . What is needed, therefore, is a continued readiness to recognize that every point of view is particular to a certain definite situation and to find out through analysis of what this particularity consists." Mannheim, as we know, believed there was one social group which was able to free itself from the influence of such particularisms: the free intelligentsia. They, he argued, could emancipate themselves from the influence of extra-cognitive circumstances so they could have a clear and undisturbed view of social reality. The free intelligentsia, therefore, were some kind of supermen who were not affected by the factors which influenced ordinary mortals.

This point of view is widely held among sociologists today: others operate in a deterministic universe while they themselves do not. The underlying belief is that sociologists are not only in a privileged social position as regards the acquisition of knowledge about social reality but also that they occupy a privileged epistemological position. When Mannheim tells us that we have to "recognize that every point of view is particular to a certain definite situation and to find out through analysis of what this particularity consists," he is presupposing the possibility of confronting a distorted image of reality (that held by others) with an image that is clear and undistorted. In other words, the epistemologically privileged position of the sociologist, by which he acquires a kind of "purified" mind, allows him access to undistorted social reality, which he can then compare with the distorted images held by others.

All sociologists who speak about studying social reality and locating regularities, variations, and interdependencies emphasize that this process is dependent on being objective and unbiased. Berelson and Steiner (1964, p. 16) remark that *"the data-collection is objective:* Once the investigation is under way, the investigator is bound to follow the data whatever way they may fall—for or against his hypothesis (however cherished), for or against his personal preferences as a man. Biased procedures in collecting data have no place in science, nor have biased perceptions of the results." Bierstedt (1963, p. 17) states that *"objectivity* means that the conclusions arrived at as the result of inquiry and investigation are independent of the race, color, creed, occupation, nationality, religion, moral preference, and political predispositions of the investigator. If his research is truly objective, it is independent of any subjective elements, any personal desires, that he may have." Riley (1963, p. 186) speaks of a *"biased viewpoint,* or failure of the researcher to perceive the facts correctly." And the English phenomenologist Silverman (1972, p. 166) stresses that it is "necessary for the observer . . . to avoid a bias in favour of his own commonsense interpretations and to seek to understand, as far as possible, the meaning(s) of the interaction to those concerned." It seems clear from the above quotations that bias and lack of objectivity are "bad" things and are to be avoided in sociological inquiry. The sociological investigator should not influence and should not be influenced by the social phenomena he studies.

Gouldner and Becker, on the other hand, argue (as I have in earlier chapters of this book) that the idea of an objective and unbiased sociology is a myth. Gouldner (1968, p. 111) speaks of the "inevitability of bias" and says that bias is "inherent in the human condition (and) in sociological research." And Becker (1967, p. 245) states that "there is no position from which sociological research can be done that is not biased in one or another way." Now one might attempt to counter these assertions by arguing that, given their point of view, we refuse to exempt them from their own accusation. For if their thesis is not exempt, we must regard their assertions as necessarily and inevitably biased. If, on the other hand, we choose to regard their thesis as correct and decide that it is not subject to the influence of one or another bias but represents an "objective" point of view, we still have problems. For, like Mannheim's sociology-of-knowledge perspective, their position is subject to the question as to why the claims that make up that perspective should be the only ones regarded as unbiased and objective.

Either there are objective truths about the social world, and Gouldner and Becker can be seen as asserting that one of these objective truths is that other sociologists are "biased" while they are not (at least with regard to that assertion); or we can take Gouldner and Becker's thesis literally and conclude that bias is inevitable and is inherent in all sociology and, indeed, in all social life. If we accept the latter alternative, however, it makes little sense to speak of bias in that nonbias or lack of bias does not exist. My point is not that one of these two alternatives represents the "right" answer or that this or that is what they "really" mean, but rather that in their two widely discussed and highly regarded essays Gouldner and Becker have left us in the dark about the nature of bias itself and why we should believe them. When Gouldner and Becker say we cannot avoid bias, or when other writers direct us to be objective and unbiased, we must ask what bias is and what it is that allows us to see bias in the first place. An interesting question, then, is not whether there is or is not bias, not whether it can be controlled or eliminated, but why we have the idea of bias itself. Sociologists do understand one another when they speak of bias and objectivity, but the extent to which they do so depends on how much they share a form of life.

Although the notions of bias and objectivity are generally taken for granted as part of the conventional wisdom of sociology, what is apparently intended in using the terms is that, in a sense, the inquirer's "self" should not be involved in the inquiry. The problem is not usually that his results can be unfavorably compared with some "pure" report on what "really" exists. Instead, the charge of bias or lack of objectivity often rests on the accusation that the findings are based, at least in part, on the character of the investigator. References are made to standards of adequate inquiry within the sociological discipline. The biased investigator violates such a standard in that his account of social reality is only one of many possible accounts. His account must be subjected to criticism so long as it is believed that there is one correct or true version of reality.

The idea of a correct version of the world implies, of course, that the sociologist has available infallible criteria for distinguishing truth from falsity. It further assumes that truth and objective knowledge are located externally, waiting to be perceived or discovered. Yet, as I have been arguing, it seems to me inescapable that truth and objective knowledge are entirely the products of social actors, and I fully share Blum's view (1970, p. 333) that "if objective knowledge is taken to mean knowledge of a reality independent of language, or presuppositionless knowledge, or knowledge of the world which is independent of the observer's procedures for finding and producing the knowledge, then there is no such thing as objective knowledge." But we can still speak of objective knowledge as long as we recognize that it is wholly a social construction. Objective knowledge exists in sociology in the sense that it is accredited by the members of the sociological community.

In speaking of sociology as a social enterprise or a form of life, I have tried to remind the reader that sociology (or any other science) requires men to agree about the ways they look at the world. Agreement is the core of the sociological enterprise; it is the quest for agreement that makes it a science. Recall the discussion in Chapter Seven concerning the views held by Popper, Peirce, Braithwaite, and Lakatos—all of whom emphasize that truth and falsity rest in Nature. Since he is cited with some frequency by sociologists, it is useful to repeat the quotation from Braithwaite (1955, pp. 53–54): "Man proposes a system of hypotheses: Nature disposes of its truth or falsity. Man invents a scientific system, and then discovers whether or not it accords with observed fact." From that point of view, sociologists are involved with discovering or locating what is in nature and comparing that reality with their theories or hypotheses. In other words, nature is the author and it is the task of sociologists to grasp nature's message. The problem for the sociological investigator, then, is to know truly about nature. He must be able to distinguish the true from the false, reality from appearance, objectivity from mere impression.

Sociology as a form of life makes a sharp distinction between truth and opinion. Membership in the sociological community rests on the rejection of opinion in the pursuit of truth. But how does the sociological inquirer *demonstrate* that he has grasped truth and that it is not merely opinion? One answer, of course, might be that he, like Mannheim's free intelligentsia, occupies a privileged epistemological position which allows him access to undistorted social reality (nature). But this is only a partial answer, for the inquirer still must communicate with other sociologists in such a manner that they will accept the adequacy of his report. A sociological community cannot exist without the possibility of agreement, and there cannot be agreement about truth and knowledge without agreement about how the sociologist should demonstrate his adequacy. If sociologists view nature as the source of truth and if they agree, as they do, that truth is not simply self-evident, to be seen just by looking, how do sociologists come to warrant the truth? Since they reject the view that some men have a direct confrontation with truth or with the speech of nature, how is it decided if one or another inquirer has grasped the truth?

The answer is that he must use the proper procedures correctly. In a sense, to be an adequate inquirer in sociology is to be "any man"— that is, to be any sociologist. Truth is "out there," authored by nature, and anyone who knows the proper procedures can grasp it. Who the inquirer is should make no difference; since truth is permanent, any sociologist can grasp it. The sociologist is merely a tool, a kind of transmission line or messenger, who relays the message or reports on the truth. Sociology is a form of life in which the adequate or good messenger is one who reports "truly," in exactly the same way that any other sociologist who knew how to see clearly would do. In fact, the individual sociologist should not be "seen" at all in his report (Raffel, 1970). Since there is only one correct report—that from nature, which the sociologist, as messenger, passes along—it should not be seen as *his* report. When it is, sociologists speak of bias and lack of objectivity. His report (or, rather, *the* report) must be indistinguishable from that of any other sociologist who has learned how to see correctly. And the only way a sociologist can demonstrate that it is not just his report, his view, his opinion, his reading of nature's message is by using the approved scientific procedures.

My arguments thus far have been directed primarily at the dominant style of sociological research—that utilizing large samples, counting, quantification, independent and dependent variables, and the like. However, I do not want to exempt other styles of sociological inquiry from consideration. I have written elsewhere (Phillips, 1971) of the importance of studying social action or meaningful behavior, a theme which has appeared in the writings of numerous sociologists since Weber. Blumer (1954, 1956, 1966), Turner (1962), and Garfinkel (1962, 1964), among others, consider interaction from the vantage point of what Wilson terms the "interpretive paradigm," within which it is viewed as "an essentially interpretive process in which meanings evolve and change over the course of interaction" (1970, p. 700). This interpretive paradigm—as found in symbolic-interactionism, ethnomethodology, and sociolinguistics—is contrasted with the "normative paradigm," in which social interaction is governed by the role expectations of the actors' respective statuses.

Although usually the differences between these two paradigms are emphasized, I wish to consider their similarities. Both paradigms are concerned with discovery. For example, Garfinkel (1967, p. viii) notes that, among other things, ethnomethodological studies are directed toward "discovering the formal properties of commonplace, practical commonsense actions"; and, in a recent book emphasizing the uniqueness of "phenomenological sociology," Phillipson (in Filmer and others, p. 94) stresses the need for a "revitalized and reformulated context of discovery." These two paradigms also share a concern with "regularities" and the like. Thus Garfinkel (1962, 1954) and Wilson (1970, p. 700) speak of the importance of documentary interpretation, which "consists of identifying an underlying pattern behind a series of appearances such that each appearance is seen as referring to, an expression of, or a 'document' of, the underlying pattern." Wilson (p. 698) recognizes that under the normative and interpretive paradigms alike, "the phenomena of interest to sociology are regularities and changes in selected features of behavior that are meaningful to the individuals involved." Thus, despite the fact that ethnomethodologists, symbolic-interactionists, and phenomenological sociologists all make much over the "methodological consequences" of their approaches, they share with the dominant approach a concern with the discovery of patterns and regularities.

They also share an emphasis on rules of procedure. Wilson (p. 706) notes that "far more careful and sophisticated attention needs to be given to the manner in which direct observations, both in field studies and in survey research, are coded." He adds further (Wilson, 1970, p. 706) that "the investigator needs to be much more explicit and self-conscious than is customary in making available to his audience the context and grounds of his interpretations." Similarly, Douglas (1970, p. 22) states: "The simple expedient of insisting on more publication of the *actual,* as opposed to idealized or reconstructed, procedures followed would help a great deal." Phillipson, speaking of participant observation, argues (in Filmer and others, 1972, p. 102): "From the phenomenological perspective the problem of participant observation is whether the observer can reconstruct for the reader what he did and how he came to select some things out as important; he must be able to demonstrate how he accomplished a level of competent performance in participant situations and the resources he employed for the accomplishment." And I have stated elsewhere, also in discussing the advantages of participant observation, that (Phillips, 1971, p. 164) "what is necessary is that the participating observer be able to provide other potential participating observers (in this case, other sociologists) with a set of explicit *instructions* (which are at present taken for granted) on how to put themselves in the same situation so as to have the same or similar experience."

Such talk of making the contexts and grounds explicit, of publishing the actual procedures followed, and of providing an explicit set of instructions refers, again, to the sociological form of life. Truth is authored by nature, and the message conveyed by one or another inquirer must be what any "competent" sociologist would convey. Therefore, the inquirer must demonstrate his competence by following the correct sociological procedures. It is as if we were all saying: "Look, this is exactly what I did, how I conducted my inquiry. Follow my instructions, do as I did, and nature will reveal to you the true message. Anyone can grasp the truth, anyone can be a good messenger, just follow my procedures—which I think are the right ones." And it is as if we might say further: "What? You followed my instructions, and nature didn't reveal the same message? You must not have followed my instructions correctly. Oh, you did, and others did as well, and none of you agrees with me? Well I guess it was just my opinion. I must have been biased after all."

This kind of thinking is a necessary consequence of a form of life which takes the audience seriously. For what all these views have in common is that their arguments are directed to a particular audience: the sociological community. All are concerned with speaking persuasively, all wish to evoke the assent of their colleagues. This communication requires a common language. This common language is the technical language, shared by all members, which speaks of variables, objectivity, patterns, regularities, taking the role of the other, documentary interpretation, and so forth. But this language and the form of life of which it is a part also involve a good deal of conventional wisdom which is considered to be normal, reasonable, and accepted as a matter of course. Sociological truth can only be warranted by an audience—the sociological community—which decides whether members have got the message straight. All of this is only to repeat the point that all science is a socially organized community of inquirers. And, as I have tried to suggest throughout this book, sociological knowledge lies in the community's methods for producing and warranting knowledge and truth.

The above discussion applies to theorizing and empirical research alike. Theory, as well as research techniques and procedures, must be correct, and deductive explanation is considered *the* scientific form of theorizing. Blum (1970, p. 307) considers this view at length and notes: "Theory is identified with correct form because in this game correct form is a condition for the production of agreement. From whom is such agreement solicited? From the collection of colleagues (scientists). Then theory is designed to produce agreement (consensus?) in one's colleagues." Blum then goes on to ask: "What kind of life would make intelligible this rock-bottom fact of needing to theorize in order to produce agreement?"

The kind of life, the form of life, which makes this emphasis on agreement necessary is one in which all men are considered equal, in the sense of being equally competent in using the proper procedures in reporting on the true account of social reality. A necessary condition for sociology as a science, then, is the securing of agreement. Thus, talk such as Smelser's about the ingredients of science—independent and dependent variables, theoretical frameworks, and research methods—serves to achieve and preserve agreement among sociologists. And the same is true of talk about the correct forms of theory, and about patterns and variations. From my point of view, what matters is not that patterns or invariances, for instance, do exist in nature but that this way of speaking allows for agreement and for community. Harre (1964, p. 32) recognizes this when he points out that "invariances are not all obvious in nature, and cannot be demonstrated in any obvious way by experiment. It is not clear how one would demonstrate experimentally that momentum is conserved in a certain sort of interaction. This cannot be done by separating off the momentum and measuring it independently of the bodies which possess it; for momentum is the product of mass and velocity and these are quite different sorts of bodily property. Clearly the origin of the invariances is not to be found in the experimental side of science. It is to be found in the general conceptual system."

Invariances, then, result from agreement or general consent within a scientific community. There can only be invariance, patterns, or whatever when there is agreement about the proper ways of doing science. Similarly, there can only be bias in sociological investigations if there can also be objectivity. Accompanying the view that truth and knowledge exist "out there" is a vision of true speech which can be communicated to the sociological community by the true messenger, one who is a tool for recording and passing on what is found in nature. Bias can only exist, can only be created, in a form of life which can speak intelligibly and understandably about nature and objectivity. Only because sociologists assume the existence of an external or objective reality, of impersonal and absolute criteria of truth and knowledge, can they speak of the "language of science."

In concluding it is useful to assert again that to conceive of sociology as a form of life is to pay attention to language. And the view of language I hold is much different from that held by either realists or nominalists, for language is neither a simple copy of "existing" structures nor an arbitrary creation of man. Rather, language develops in the midst of human communities, whose members can change or modify it through using it. In doing so, they must appeal to reasoning or argumentation for justifying these changes or modifications. Reasoning and argumentation cannot, however, be employed when one holds the realist or nominalist point of view, which gives language no purchase of its own. To see this, let me briefly consider these two viewpoints.

For the realists, our notions correspond to external essences which exist as self-evident truths to be discovered by use of our rational faculties. Meanings are given by reason or intuition, and the key to truth is given by pure thought—of which logic and mathematics are often considered representative. Thus, it is not experience or the senses but pure conceptual analysis which allows for indubitable judgments about reality. The nominalist viewpoint, on the other hand, emphasizes that meanings are given by experience, ultimately reducible to sense data. Experience can establish an immediate contact between subject and object. The emphasis in the modern versions of nominalism and empiricism—logical positivism, pragmatism, and operationalism—is on observation and empirical evidence. Contemporary sociology contains both realist and nominalist elements. It is nominalistic in the sense that it does not accept the derivation of synthetic propositions from given rational ideas as constituting definitive evidence for its empirical validity. But it follows the realist doctrine in so far as it regards rational ideas as guiding principles in making predictions that are then tested by observation.

For realists, language is simply a copy of preestablished structures; while for the nominalists, language is used to order our experiences. The concepts of our language allow us to order the individual observable facts making up the world. Thus, from the nominalist perspective, language is arbitrarily conceived by man. It has no importance of its own, because the same experiences are expressible in different languages, all quite interchangeable. Therefore, nominalism and realism alike can be viewed as trying to eliminate language, in that it is considered a factor of distortion and misunderstanding with regard to the basis of truth and knowledge. Palmer (1969, p. 230), who rejects the theory of language as basically an instrument of communication, puts it nicely: "Language is not man's means of putting wordless thoughts and wordless experiences into a form to which he has assigned a meaning; thinking, understanding, and experience are all completely linguistic, for it is through language that one has the world of understanding in and through which objects take their place in his experience."

Although sociologists proceed as if we had access to a neutral, extra-linguistic means of reporting, of talking about truth and knowledge, it seems preferable to recognize that there is no knowledge that is objective or impersonal or guaranteed by a divine mind. Sociological truth and knowledge are human phenomena and are to be found in the cultural milieu, in the tradition, in the form of life of sociology itself.

★★★★★★★★★★★★★★★★

9

Abandoning Method

★★★★★★★★★★★★★★★★

In this chapter I pursue a theme introduced in the previous chapter: the consequences for sociological practice of an emphasis on community. This emphasis results in a dependence on method as a condition of membership. And while method may have a unifying effect and provide a kind of collective protection for a discipline's practitioners, it restricts the freedom of the individual scientist. The central thesis of this chapter, therefore, is that the abandonment of method may be a necessary condition for improving our knowledge and our lives.

Let me begin by pointing out that scientists often lay heavy stress on the differences between themselves and those whom they study. Schutz (1970), Garfinkel (1967), Cicourel (1964), and Gouldner (1970) have all been highly critical of this attitude, arguing that there is less difference between the sociologist and those he studies than the sociologist seems to think. Like the sociologist, those being studied have their own social theories, conduct investigations, and are also frequently involved in using various methodological procedures for testing those theories. Given these similarities, we might wonder what is so special about the sociologist.

The major characteristic distinguishing the sociologist from the layman, I think, is that he belongs to a specific scientific community with other men and women who are also regarded as sociologists. But what is it *about* his membership that separates him from the layman, who may also share his interest in religious behavior, birth rates, family living patterns, the "causes" of crime, and the like? To answer this question, we must consider the nature of a scientific community.

The professional, unlike the layman, generally possesses a special credential, awarded by the gatekeepers of the profession as evidence that he has acquired the requisite knowledge and skills to be considered a full-fledged member. In the United States, especially, this credential takes the form of a Ph.D. degree—a necessary prerequisite for teaching in the "best" colleges and the "major" universities. To acquire this precious document, the average sociologist spends about ten years between his bachelor's and doctor's degrees (Smelser and Davis, 1969, p. 138).

Having spent all those years studying sociology (and in some instances he may have spent part of the four years necessary for his bachelor's degree studying sociology as well), he is thought to have acquired a certain unique knowledge and special skills. He is supposed to know more about social phenomena than the layman. I have already indicated my skepticism that sociologists possess any unique knowledge with regard to understanding society, successfully predicting future events, cataloging social laws, and the like. And let me also register my disbelief with regard to the so-called humanizing influence of most sociology courses. What the sociologist does generally possess that distinguishes him from the layman is an enormous amount of "information." He is certainly more likely than the average person to know about Marx, Weber, Durkheim, Parsons, Merton, Gouldner, Goffman, Habermas, and other past and present luminaries. I do not mean to denigrate the possession of such information but only to emphasize that a major part of becoming a sociologist consists in learning who said what about this or that. The sociologist is also more likely than most laymen to be acquainted with certain "facts": that there is, for example, an increase in the number of Puerto Ricans living in New York City, or a decrease in church attendance in the United States, or that certain occupations are accorded greater prestige in the Netherlands than in Japan. In addition, the sociologist is supposed to have special evidence to explain why lower-class persons are more (or less) authoritarian than other people, or why Catholics have more children than non-Catholics, or whatever. But, as I have noted in earlier chapters, this special evidence is not very impressive, whether judged by the sociologist's own criteria or that of the disinterested (or hostile) critic. In short, it is extremely difficult to locate any special expertise possessed by the sociologist which will clearly and definitively distinguish him from the layman. Granted that he may have a great amount of information about various social phenomena, but I have yet to see a justification for the establishment and maintenance of the discipline of sociology which laid particular emphasis on the possession of information.

As I attempted to show in the previous chapter, however, the sociologist differs radically from other people in his form of life: the language he uses, the way he carves up the world, and the manner in which he and his fellows go about deciding what is and is not to be accepted as constituting knowledge. The sociologist, like every other scientist, wants to communicate with a specific audience. The sociologist and the layman often ask the same questions about the social world, they both have theories, and they both conduct investigations. And both frequently ask themselves and others: "How do you know?" But whereas the layman is usually satisfied with a biographical answer, the sociologist demands what might be called a logical answer (see Toulmin, 1969). For instance, the layman might answer the question "How do you know that Catholics have more children than Protestants?" by replying: "My Catholic neighbors all have more children than my Protestant ones" or "I know because I read it in the newspaper." In other words, he answers by indicating how he came to be in a position to speak about whatever is at issue. The sociologist, on the other hand, is expected to answer such a question by citing the grounds (evidence, justification, proof) for his assertion. He must be prepared to appeal to the agreed-upon criteria within the scientific community for warranting sociological knowledge. Because he wishes to evoke the assent of other sociologists, to speak persuasively to them, he must emphasize the "correct" sociological methods. I described earlier the nature and uses of these methods. Further, I have argued that notions such as truth, bias, objectivity, and validity can only exist within a certain form of life, which is, in many respects, shared by all scientific communities. But I have yet to say anything about why method (by which I refer to various theories and conventions, as well as methodological techniques and procedures) plays such a definitive role in sociology.

The major reason why method is so central to sociology, and the reason why it is the major factor which distinguishes the writings and assertions of the sociologist from those of the layman, is that sociology, like any other scientific discipline, requires some explicit, shared, agreed on criteria for evaluating the work of those within the discipline. In some sciences it is probably enough that their results seem to "work" (as with the substantive results of physics, chemistry, biology, and perhaps economics among the social sciences). In sociology, however, it is enormously difficult to evaluate the results of various inquiries. But in all science it is necessary to tell the scientist from the fake, the charlatan from the real, the true guide from the false one. In science, as in democracy, there is always a need for some rules by which the worst tendencies of others will be checked and balanced. By placing a heavy emphasis on correct method, all members of a scientific community are assured a kind of collective protection: madmen, charlatans, fakers, and sophists are hopefully excluded from the ranks.

During the history of sociology, certain widely shared methodological assumptions associated with positivism have united such diverse sociological practitioners as Comte and Marx, Weber and Durkheim, Parsons and Garfinkel, Merton and Becker. All, in varying degrees, believe that by observation, classification of data, and testing, social phenomena can be made to yield laws like those found in the more exact sciences. They further agree that the laws governing social phenomena are discoverable, although they differ somewhat as to the proper methods for assuring such discoveries. But whatever their versions of proper method, they all believe that correct method will guarantee the power to predict the future course of events.

This emphasis developed partially because of a preoccupation among social thinkers with community. Wolin (1960, pp. 363–364) notes that "the political and social thought of the nineteenth and twentieth centuries largely centered on the attempt to restate the value of community, that is, of the need for human beings to dwell in more intimate relationships with each other, to enjoy more affective ties, to experience some closer solidarity than the nature of urbanized and industrialized society seemed willing to grant." Comte, Tonnies, Weber, Durkheim, and Saint-Simon were all explicitly concerned with problems of community. Saint-Simon, especially, stressed organization as a means of promoting the kinds of social relationships required for community. What men could not do individually they could accomplish by collective organization. Weber (1947, p. 337), one of the first to systematically consider that matter of organization, had this to say about bureaucracy: "The whole pattern of everyday life is cut to fit this framework. For bureaucratic administration is . . . always from a formal, technical point of view the most rational type. For the needs of mass administration today, it is completely indispensable. The choice is only that between bureaucracy and dilettantism in the field of administration." Concern with social control and stability also underlay the emphasis on organization. In *Suicide,* Durkheim stressed that in all realms of life men had come to accept lack of organization as normal. For Durkheim, the restoration of group life was the remedy for this disorganization. "Collective representations are the result of an immense cooperation which stretches out not only into space but into time as well; to make them, a multitude of minds have associated, united and combined their ideas and sentiments; for them, long generations have accumulated their experience and their knowledge" (1915, p. 16). To Durkheim, the community had prior reality, and in nineteenth-century social thought it was the community that held the attention of leading social theorists. Instead of man being primary and social relationships secondary, the order was reversed.

The desire for community, for more intimate relationships, for people to in some way unite with one another had obvious repercussions for the various sciences. For if there are to be scientific "communities," it is necessary to minimize or eliminate individual idiosyncracies and peculiarities. To be a good scientist, just as to be a good citizen, one's loyalty must be to community. If every scientist were to go his own way, using his own particular methods and arriving at his own truths, community would be impossible. However, in a true community, men could unite through various forms of organization. And in science, they could do this by following certain prescribed methods. Since all members of the scientific community are, in the sense described in the last chapter, considered equal and have equal access to nature's messages, the right method will yield identical results for the genius and mediocrity alike. Thus, an emphasis on method serves to create and maintain community, as well as providing a kind of collective protection against the fake or charlatan. Perhaps partially because sociology was launched as a science of the aggregate, it has long been the most methodologically self-conscious of the social sciences. Consider Durkheim's statement (1949, p. 26): "A group is not only a moral authority which dominates the life of its members; it is also a source of life *sui generis*. From it comes a warmth which animates its members, making them intensely human, destroying their egotisms." For Durkheim, the group, the association, the community became not only the focus of sociological attention but the framework of analysis within which religion, law, and so forth were to be understood. Community reality precedes the individual, who is to be considered only an abstraction.

The functionalist strain in Durkheim and in much sociology since his time also probably encourages the emphasis on method and community, in that it expresses a rather obvious hostility toward individualism. Durkheim stresses that the individual conscience must be subordinate to the collective conscience, and he warns us that "to fight against nature we need more vigorous faculties and more productive strength. . . . We rather see perfection in the man seeking, not to be complete, but to produce. . . . In one of its aspects, the categorical imperative of the moral conscience is assuming the following form: Make yourself usefully fulfill a determinate function" (quoted in Wolin, 1960, p. 387). The proper role of the sociologist, then, like that of any other individual, is the performance of a determinate function. No wonder an emphasis on method has come to serve as the main unifying force in maintaining the community of sociological practitioners.

But concern with method also stultifies the individual,

dampens his strongest passions, and molds him to the requirements for membership in the scientific community. Most of all, however, correct method may block him from confronting experience and restrict his imagination. It limits possibility, it prevents him from realizing what might have been, and while it provides security, it eliminates certain sources of excitement from his intellectual life. Although the emphasis on correct method seems especially pronounced in sociology, it is sufficiently widespread in all sciences to have come under heavy attack by Paul Feyerabend in his provocative article "Against Method."

Anarchistic Methodology

Feyerabend (1970, p. 17) begins by asserting that "*anarchism,* while perhaps not the most attractive *political* philosophy, is certainly an excellent foundation for *epistemology,* and for the *philosophy of science.*" He goes on to criticize the notion of correct method (pp. 19–20): "For nobody can say in abstract terms, without paying attention to idiosyncrasies of person and circumstances, what precisely it was that led to progress in the past, and nobody can say what moves will succeed in the future." And he asserts further (pp. 21–22):

The idea of a method that contains firm, unchanging, and absolutely binding principles for conducting the business of science gets into considerable difficulty when confronted with the results of historical research. We find, then, that there is not a single rule, however plausible, and however firmly grounded in epistemology, that is not violated at some time or other. It becomes evident that such violations are not accidental events, they are not the results of insufficient knowledge or of inattention which might have been avoided. On the contrary, we see that they are necessary for progress. Indeed, one of the most striking features of recent discussions in the history and philosophy of science is the realization that developments such as the Copernican Revolutions, or the rise of atomism in antiquity and recently (kinetic theory; dispersion theory; stereochemistry; quantum theory), or the gradual emergence of the wave theory of light occurred either because some thinkers decided *not to be bound by certain "obvious" methodological rules or because they* unwittingly broke *them.*

The major principle of his "anarchistic" methodology is that *anything goes.* Among other things, adherence to this principle leads him to reject the rule that agreement between theory and data should be regarded as favoring the theory while disagreement endangers the theory or causes it to be eliminated altogether; instead he suggests (p. 26) that we introduce and elaborate hypotheses which are inconsistent either with well-established theories or with well-established facts. This maneuver he terms proceeding "counterinductively." He also advocates a principle of "proliferation," by which we invent and elaborate "theories" which are inconsistent with accepted points of view. He regards these two principles as essential parts of any critical science.

Feyerabend argues that the principle of proliferation is an essential aspect of a humanitarian outlook. He notes that progressive educators have always attempted to develop the individuality of their pupils while, at the same time, preparing them for the "realities" of life. Usually, he points out, this interpretation means that they must learn one particular set of views—those pertaining to what is considered reality—to the general exclusion of other views, especially those seen as having their proper application in the world of art or less "practical" matters. Feyerabend is critical of the belief that fantasy and imagination are regarded as suitable only for art and not for real-world concerns and asks (p. 27) whether this will not lead to a split between "a hated reality and welcome fantasies, science and the arts, careful description and unrestrained self-expression?" Not, he answers, if we regard the principle of proliferation as a kind of creative device. He stresses the importance of retaining the freedom of artistic creation in discovering and changing the world we live in.

Play

Feyerabend's opposition to method and his advocacy of counterinduction and proliferation suggest the importance of playful activities—those not guided by formal rules or methods but engaged in for themselves. Play is existence centered in itself. Both play in the usual sense and proliferation as a kind of play-form help to assure our freedom so that we can decide (if initially only in fantasy) the way we want to live our lives and develop our talents, rather than adopting by habit or following proper methods.

It is important here to distinguish my conception of play from that formulated by other sociologists. Simmel (1950) and Goffman (1961), for example, both devote considerable attention to play as a form of interaction. Thus Simmel (1950, pp. 42–43) speaks of the numerous phenomena that we lump together under the category of play: "Actual forces, needs, impulses of life produce the forms of our behavior that are suitable for play. These forms, however, become independent contents and stimuli within play itself or, rather, *as* play. There are, for instance, the hunt; the gain by ruse; the proving of physical and intellectual strength; competition; and the dependence on chance and on the favor of powers that cannot be influenced." And regarding sociability as the play-form of sociation, Simmel (p. 45) emphasizes that "inasmuch as in the purity of its manifestation, sociability has no objective purpose, no content, no extrinsic results, it entirely depends on the personalities among whom it occurs. Its aim is nothing but the success of the sociable moment and, at most, a memory of it." Sociability, then, is a kind of game. At a party, for example, we may *play at* competition, cooperation, love, hostility, deceit, and numerous other social behaviors.

This formulation of play is clearly *rule*-governed, in that it is concerned with social interaction. And while there are differences between serious and playful interaction, both depend on rules. There are rules covering linguistic conventions, courtship, parenthood, religious worship, friendship, and so on. There are rules covering certain games (tennis, football, chess, for example). All of this is rather obvious, perhaps. But what might be somewhat less obvious is that there are also conventions for such playful activities as kidding or flirting, although these rules may not be explicitly formulated. A man who "flirts" with a woman at a party by ripping off her clothes and throwing her to the floor will almost certainly be seen as exceeding the rules of flirting. For the notion of flirting involves conducting oneself according to certain social agreements. With varying degrees of self-consciousness, all people consider rules in their interactions with others. In short, all social life is regulated by rules.

Since I am trying to formulate play as something standing in opposition to rules and methods, the usual sociological formulations of play are inadequate here. For me, play is a viable alternative to method only if it can be viewed as an individual or private activity, engaged in for its own sake and not because of a concern with other persons. That is, play, as I am using the term here, is not rule-governed and is not methodical. Daydreaming, for instance, is not rule-governed. There are no "correct" or "right" ways to daydream. In fact, daydreaming may be viewed, sympathetically or not, as something which puts the individual outside of ordinary, everyday, rule-governed, social intercourse. It is a truly solitary activity.

Most people, I imagine, view play as standing in opposition to work, to science, to utility, to reality, to seriousness. Of course, we are usually told that sociology (and all science) is an extremely serious enterprise and that we, like the child with his education, should concern ourselves with "reality." Given the view that social facts should be studied as things standing outside the observer, reality is considered that which is external, discrete, tangible, quantifiable, and susceptible to being conveyed to other sociologists in a precise manner. Since science is the epitome of rationality, it should be conducted with a heavy emphasis on objectivity and adherence to method. A realistic and tough-minded attitude toward the real world is the goal. That which might be subjective or touched by feeling has no place in scientific sociology. Although science, including sociology, occupies a kind of sacred position in the eyes of many, we must remember that sociology—and whatever standards it imposes on us—is our own creation. The idea that it should be run according to some fixed rules and methods, and that we must follow them, need not be accepted. We can try to turn our eyes and our minds in new directions. And I would suggest that one way is by considering the usefulness of play.

Plato, in many of his writings, exalted the concept of play to the highest regions of the spirit. For example, in the *Republic,* we find (1969: vii: 536):

Now, all this study of reckoning and geometry and all the preliminary studies that are indispensable preparation for dialectic must be presented to them while still young, not in the form of compulsory education.

Why so?

Because, said I, a free soul ought not to pursue any study slavishly, for while bodily labors performed under constraint do not harm the body, nothing that is learned under compulsion stays with the mind.

True, he said.

Do not, then, my friend, keep children to their studies by compulsion but by play. That will also better enable you to discern the natural capacities of each.

And in the *Laws* (1969: vii: 803), we are instructed: "All of us, then men and women alike, must fall in with our role and spend life in making our *play* as perfect as possible." In his view, then, "true" learning and education come from play. Freud (1959, pp. 173–174) also emphasized the importance of play: "We ought surely to look in the child for the first sources of imaginative activity. The child's best loved and most absorbing occupation is play. Perhaps we may say that every child at play behaves like an imaginative writer, in that he creates a world of his own, or, more truly, he rearranges the things of his world and orders it in a new way that pleases him better."

Hegel, Schiller, Nietzsche, and Heidegger all considered the importance of play. And Marx spoke of work as preventing the worker from finding pleasure in the play of his own bodily and intellectual forces. More recently, Huizinga (1962) has stressed the necessity of play for man's development. In his *Homo Ludens* (1962, p. 13) he discusses the characteristics of play and concludes: "Summing up the formal characteristics of play we might call it a free activity, standing quite consciously outside 'ordinary' life as being 'not serious' but at the same time absorbing the player intensely and utterly." It involves a fuller use of the imagination than is found in such serious pursuits as, for instance, sociology. Speaking of the child at play, Huizinga (pp. 13–14) states: "The child is *making an image* of something different, something more beautiful, or more sublime, or more dangerous than what he usually *is.*" Among the ancient Greeks this same notion of play formed the basis of the Hellenic idea of education and culture. Whereas science imposes on its practitioners certain fixed rules and standards, playful activities give free rein to intuition and imagination, to what is, in McWilliams' words, "subjective, fleshy, and private in man" (1970, p. 372).

Though Huizinga's analysis of play is the most extended that I know of, like most writers on the subject he denigrates play by contrasting it with "reality." That is, he assumes the existence of a reality, that this reality exists prior to play, and that play occurs against this background of what is real. Especially in advanced, industrial societies, play is often viewed as having no consequences for real life, as opposed to the seriousness of real life, as wasted time, producing nothing. Science and work, it is argued, result in a product and transform the world, while play has no grasp of—and stands apart from—the real world. Even those writing sympathetically about play often see it as a kind of temporal oasis, interrupting the continuity and purposive structure of our lives. But why should reality serve as the standard for play?

Play is different from the usual and the everyday in that it is not engaged in for the sake of some final goal. Whereas with most activities, we live anticipating the future and view the present as simply preparation for "what comes next," play has only an internal purpose, unrelated to anything external to itself. But the fact that play is different is no reason to grant precedence to reality (or seriousness) over play. We might say that people play because they are people, thus suggesting that play has precedence over reality or seriousness. But this statement too is misleading, for play is an aspect of the reality which men construct. In a sense, then, to discuss play is to discuss reality. Thus, while I speak of play as distinguished from method, I do so only to identify an aspect of social reality which is frequently ignored. I do believe that play is the ultimate manifestation of human freedom and self-determinism and that it allows man to realize a kind of human sovereignty. But I do not consider play as something unreal.

Perhaps a playful approach to sociological inquiry would

allow us to confront our own experience, to pay attention to what we have seen, heard, felt, and wondered about, and to what we already know. By assuming a more playful stance, we can perhaps free ourselves from the dogmatism of method. Play, by freeing us from a heavy dependence on method, may enable us to confront the world without the scientific "blinders" required for membership in the sociological community. Play may not only give free rein to imagination, intuition, and creative urges, but may help us see more clearly. Because method, in a sense, enslaves us, we surrender our freedom when we accept method—at least as it is dictated by the scientific community. Of course, method is inevitable and inescapable, in the sense that we all employ various theories and conduct our investigations in going about our everyday lives. And we could not function as human beings without a reliance on various methods, although they need not be those prescribed by the sociological community.

I suggest that a playful attitude is a necessary precondition for "experiencing" the world. Now, I do not mean only that which we call experience in life (although that too is obviously important), but something which might be termed "deep" experience. There is a kind of taken-for-granted experience which constitutes the routine and ordinary happenings or aspects of our lives. But there is also a deeper sense of the term; as Hegel argues, experience always has the structure of reversing or restructuring awareness. It is a dialectical kind of movement. As Gadamer (in Palmer, 1969, p. 196) puts it: "Every experience runs counter to expectation if it really deserves the name experience." In order to realize a reversal, a restructuring, or a counter-expectation—that is, to realize experience in the deep sense—we must allow ourselves the possibility of seeing things as if for the first time. We must free ourselves from the customary, the ordinary, the usual if we are to see things as new and unrecognized.

Often what we know best, most deeply and truly, is what we have directly experienced ourselves. We often understand what a certain phenomenon "means" because we, ourselves, have experienced it. To understand what something means is the major goal of sociology, but it is also the fundamental role of existence for the human species. Understanding is heightened when there can be experience, openness, and a willingness to let the phenomenon lead. Method is antithetical to the openness of experience, while play is not.

Gouldner seems to be expressing a similar point of view when he discusses self-knowing and self-reflection (1972, p. 19): "When the normal sociologist encounters a problem, his first impulse is to put on his hat, shoes, and coat and to leave at once, to go somewhere, anywhere, as long as it is somewhere else, to go into the 'field' and to probe and prod the 'out there.' The normal sociologist's deepest dogma is fundamentally *externalizing.*" As antidote, Gouldner proposes (p. 19) that "what he should do first, and do with careful thoroughness, is to *think* about the thing and to talk with colleagues and comrades. Higher and prior to research there is *reflection.* The sociologist should first conduct a dialogue with himself and with others to see what he already knows-believes about the matter at issue and then critically evaluate the results this produces."

I completely agree with everything Gouldner says here, but I would apply the directive before the sociologist first encounters a specific problem. I advocate playful activity as often a necessary preliminary to encountering one or another problem of inquiry. In other words, play may allow him to free himself of the presuppositions which determine what he, as a sociologist, will view as a problem. We need to make ourselves focally aware of those things which have only our subsidary attention. We should draw upon what Polanyi (1958) calls our "tacit awareness" of our experiences. We must try to make our tacit knowledge explicit in such a way that we are able to reflect upon it.

Since I have spoken at length about play, the reader may have an image of the adult sociologist sitting like a child among his toys or aimlessly throwing a ball back and forth. While this might not always be such a bad idea, it is not what I have in mind. Rather, I mean activity that is not usually directed toward some specified end: it is engaged in for itself. Quite clearly, it is much different from building a theory or conducting a scientific investigation. Play is not "for" something, although it is often the closest that most of us will ever come to engaging in pure speculation. Bakunin once exclaimed (Carr, 1937, pp. 8–9): "Let people emancipate themselves and they will instruct themselves of their own accord."

If people are free of rules, methods, and a dependence on correct procedures, they will instruct themselves. Take away the program and people will find a way.

Implicit in all the above, of course, is an assumption that man is by nature curious, that he wants to understand himself and the world around him. I do believe this to be the case. I do believe that most young children are enormously curious about the world and their surroundings, that they want to know about all kinds of things. As Bertrand Russell (1961, p. 425) noted, "The instinctive foundation of the intellectual life is curiosity. . . . Animals, machines, thunderstorms, and all forms of manual work arouse the curiosity of children, whose thirst for knowledge puts the most intelligent adult to shame." The most important thing about the child's curiosity is that it is *his* and serves *him*. It is not responsible to the demands of one or another community. The child wants to know, he wants to understand, and in his playful activities he allows his curiosity full sway. But the adult, and here we must consider again the scientist, must subject himself to method. Curiosity and play are not subject to method, but rather to thought. It is in the nature of man to want to know and to understand what is. To be fully human and fully alive, the individual must give his highest loyalty to thought.

Instead of letting method guide thought, we must remember that method, whether in sociology or elsewhere, has been created by thought. What is important, then, is not theory, not method (in the narrower sense of rules and techniques), but thought itself. Thought, in the sense of playful curiosity most especially, is responsible only to itself. Adherence to method prevents us from imagining things as otherwise than they are, from viewing the world in a different manner.

Other Audiences

I have emphasized throughout the past few chapters that sociological knowledge is not something lying out there to be "discovered," although that is the task that most sociologists see themselves as pursuing. Rather, knowledge is created or constructed by members of the sociological community, and it is to be found in the form of life of sociology itself. I have argued further that sociological conceptions of truth and knowledge depend on a view of nature as the big author in the sky and rely on the scientific community as the arbiter of truth and knowledge. Whether one believes that truth and knowledge have to do with correspondence to the "facts" or that they are determined by compliance with the requirements of correct method, he must allow the scientific community to make the final judgment as to the truth or falsity of his claims. The decision and consensus of the community determine sociological truth and knowledge. If there were no sociological community, there could be no scientific knowledge about social phenomena.

It is important to stress the term *scientific,* for we can imagine ourselves—even without the existence of a sociological community (though not without human society)—possessing practical knowledge. We can conceive of understanding and knowing about things, although this knowledge would not be considered scientific (or even "knowledge") unless it were warranted as such by the relevant professional community.

Many writers have discussed the importance of audience or community, but their emphasis has been somewhat different from mine. Merton (1957, p. 362), for example, states:

> *A basic concept which serves to differentiate generalizations about the thoughts and knowledge of an entire society or culture is that of the "audience" or "public" or what Znaniecki calls "the social circle." Men of knowledge do not orient themselves exclusively toward their data nor toward the total society, but to special segments of that society with their special demands, criteria of validity, of significant knowledge, or pertinent problems, etc. It is through anticipation of these demands and expectations of particular audiences, which can be effectively located in the social structure, that men of knowledge organize their own work, define their data, seize upon problems.*

Ziman (1968, p. 9), in *Public Knowledge: The Social Dimension of Science,* also stresses the importance of audience: "The objective of Science is not just to acquire information nor to utter all noncontradictory notions; its goal is a consensus of rational opinion over the widest possible field. . . . The audience to which scientific publications are addressed is not passive; by its cheering and booing, its bouquets or brickbats, it actively controls the substance of the communications that it receives." While both Merton and Ziman stress the audience or community to which scientists orient themselves, and from which they receive their problems, theories, methods, and rewards, they fail to see that scientific truth or knowledge exist *only* by virtue of being warranted by the scientific community.

There can be no sociological knowledge without community, and there can be no community without method. Only insofar as certain methods are shared as the correct ones for conducting investigations and warranting knowledge can we speak of a community and, hence, of a science. No method, no community; no community, no science. Realization of this relation has helped give rise to the various sciences and "schools" of science over the centuries, as men searched for and created new intellectual communities which emphasized different methods to which they could more comfortably accommodate themselves. The search for a new and better sociological community can be witnessed in Gouldner's remarks (1972, p. 56) concerning the social theorist: "The theorist as theorist should commit himself to the establishment of *his own* social collective to know intellectually and to create practically the conditions requisite for national discourse and human liberation and within whose protection he and his fellows work toward the understanding of the concrete social totality with which they are historically faced."

These are indeed noble sentiments, but they still seem to place the individual sociologist in a position of dependence on the community—"our own social collective"—as regards such questions as whether the individual scholar has reached an "understanding of the concrete social totality." The answers must involve method, for issues of method play a part in any science. Thus the sociologist can trade one community for another, thereby changing the methods by which he will be restrained, but he cannot avoid the dictates of method so long as he is part of a sociological community. What he can try to do, however, is to stop thinking of himself as a technical specialist or professional and consider other audiences than those consisting entirely of sociologists. By conceiving of himself and his interests less narrowly, he can attempt to avoid the extreme compartmentalization which characterizes present-day science.

Since Durkheim, many sociologists have seen reality as divided into several series of *sui generis* phenomena: physical, biological, psychic, social, and so on. Such divisions have helped to produce the disciplinary boundaries I discussed earlier. The result has been the creation of autonomous disciplines, which often seem unaware that the "same" phenomena can be studied by psychology, history, or philosophy, as well as by sociology. Criticism of such occupational specialization is not new. It runs through the writings of Marx and Engels, who believed that every social division of labor is an enemy of human freedom (1947, p. 22): "For as soon as labor is distributed, each man has a particular exclusive sphere of activity, which is forced upon him and from which he cannot escape. He is a hunter, a fisherman, a shepherd, or a social critic, and must remain so if he does not want to lose his means of livelihood."

While Marx and Engels were speaking specifically about a division of labor under which men are compelled by economic necessity to occupational specialization, I believe that the division of labor represented by the various scientific disciplines also creates a loss of intellectual freedom. It is in the very nature of specialization to restrict the possibilities for our understanding and knowing about those things that concern us. When we say that such-and-such is a "philosophical" or "psychological" or "sociological" problem, we display our unwillingness and inability to let the problem guide us. Of course, it is impossible for any one of us to be familiar with all of the various social sciences or with philosophy and history. But were we to conceive of ourselves as social thinkers, or theorists, or intellectuals, or almost any other category of inquirer, rather than as members of one or another profession, we might be more willing and better able to extend our horizons of inquiry.

It seems to me that a good writer or journalist does this anyhow. He takes as his audience a wide spectrum of intelligent readers. And instead of being guided in his presentation by a narrow notion of correct method, he relies entirely on speech itself. The criterion for his argument is whether or not his speech is intelligible. But because he does not depend heavily on method, whatever he might say is bound to be more disputable than what is said by those who are guided by explicit considerations of method. Reliance on method is always more directed at eliciting agreement than is the speech of the writer who has in mind a less specialized audience. Those whose allegiance is to a specific discipline must undergo an initiation into the corpus of doctrine and into the methods regarded as valid for that discipline.

This scientific view creates a clear separation between theory and practice, between scientific truths and the opinions that guide our action. The answers we give to the questions posed by practical life are not worked out by rigid adherence to the methods of science, nor are they based on adherence to the laws of deductive logic. This is not to say, however, that these answers are the results of completely arbitrary decisions. Rather, we have *reasons* for making one or another decision. Similarly, in sociological inquiry, we take an audience into account when offering our explanations. If we follow the rules stipulated beforehand and *demonstrate* that the methods have been correctly followed, the audience will agree with and endorse the truth of the assertion. The alternative to this dependence on method and demonstration—an alternative usually ignored or denigrated by men who consider themselves scientists—is to employ and rely on reasoning and *argumentation.* (I owe this distinction to Perelman, 1963.)

Opinions and Arguments

There has long existed in the social sciences a controversy concerning two opposite methodological approaches to the study of social phenomena. One emphasizes the methodological unity of the natural and social sciences; the other stresses the subjective quality of social phenomena and argues that the social sciences require different methods of inquiry from those used in natural science investigations. The *erklären* and *verstehen* methods, as these are often called, are seen as competitors for the proper study of mankind. And while subscribers to the *verstehen* persuasion are generally unwilling to concede a place for covering-law explanations (the *erklären* tradition), those emphasizing *erklären* do consider *verstehen*—but only as a useful heuristic device or as a source of hunches or insights. Hempel and Oppenheim (1953, p. 330), for example, speak of *verstehen,* or "understanding," as follows: "[U]nderstanding . . . in terms of one's own psychological function may prove a useful heuristic device in the search for general psychological principles which might provide a theoretical explanation: but the existence of empathy on the part of the scientist is neither a necessary nor a sufficient condition for explanation, or the scientific understanding, of any human action."

Unfortunately, they miss the point of what Max Weber, at least, seemed to intend when speaking of *verstehen.* So does Abel, who offers the following example with regard to the usefulness of *verstehen* in understanding the relationship between marriage and crop production (1948, p. 217): "We do not accept the fact that farmers postpone intended marriages when faced with crop failures because we can 'understand' the connection. This is acceptable to us because we have found through reliable statistical operations that the correlation between the rate of marriage and the rate of crop production is extremely high. We would continue to accept the fact even if we could not 'understand' it." Abel's remarks, however, pertain to only one of the two types of *verstehen* considered by Weber. Abel is speaking only of *erklärendes verstehen,* which, according to Weber (1963, p. 142), is achieved when "the behavior in question can be designated as part of an understandable sequence of emotions." But Weber also spoke of *aktuelles verstehen,* which concerns the understanding of the meaning of a given act. Whereas *erklärendes verstehen* pertains to understanding "why," *aktuelles verstehen* refers to understanding "what" someone is doing. If we consider both types of *verstehen,* instead of only the one focused on by Hempel, Abel, and most other writers on the subject, we can see an obvious weakness in many criticisms of *verstehen.* Abel says that we would continue to accept the fact of the correlation between crop production and rates of marriage even if we could not understand it. However, unless we understand in Weber's sense of *aktuelles verstehen,* we would have no notion of what counts as marriage or crop failure or high correlation. Abel fails to recognize that marriage, crop production, failure, and so on are social constructs. Without understanding *what they mean* (how they are used in a particular form of life), we would have only a correlation (if we knew what that was) between something and something else. Weber

(1947, pp. 99–100) himself pointed this out when he stated: "If adequacy in respect to meaning is lacking then no matter how high the degree of uniformity and how precisely its probability can be numerically determined it is still an incomprehensible statistical probability whether dealing with overt or subjective processes." Thus, contrary to the views of Hempel and Oppenheim (1953), Abel (1948), Parsons (1949), and Hughes (1961), *verstehen* is not simply a source of hunches or a generator of hypotheses. It is rather the sine qua non for understanding man's behavior. Unless we understand how those who are the subjects of our inquiry construct their social worlds, unless we are familiar with their commonsense constructs and experiences, we cannot engage in any type of meaningful sociological explanation. Therefore, a certain conception of *verstehen* is, I believe, crucial for sociological inquiry.

There is another mode of inquiry which is not dependent on the usual *erklären-verstehen* methodological approaches. In the following discussion I consider reasoning and argumentation and discuss two aspects of this emphasis: that concerned with accounting for or explaining social phenomena and that involving the sociologist's relations with an audience. In the previous chapter I criticized the view that explanations must rest on generalities (laws) for their support. I pointed out that sociologists exempt themselves from the influence of causal laws. Toulmin (1970b, p. 1) puts the problem nicely:

> *On the one hand, scientists have extended the scope of categories like* body *and* matter, physical *and* mechanical, *into ever larger areas of the natural world; and each new extension has seemingly subjected further kinds of phenomenon and system to the reign of "causal necessity." On the other hand, all men—scientists and non-scientists alike—have continued to think and act, take stands, criticize each other and justify themselves; and have cited as the factors relevant to an understanding of their conduct, not the physical or mechanical* causes *underlying their actions, but rather the* reasons *for which they acted as they did.*

In sociology, not only large-scale quantitative studies but also those relying on most versions of *verstehen*—where the investigator tries to explain human action by plumbing the motives of those whom he investigates—warrant an explanation as adequate when it can be shown that the account can be extended beyond the case in question. Furthermore, such studies are directed toward discovering some underlying pattern, motives, causes, or functions. As against this mode of explanation (which I have considered at length in Chapter Eight), I want to suggest that human behavior is explained by presenting arguments which justify the behavior in question. This procedure does not involve discovering patterns or laws or anything else, but is rather a matter of putting forth possible ways of viewing some aspects of the social world.

Thus I would not speak, for instance, of Freud's discovering the unconscious or of Marx's discovering the influence of the modes of production in society. Instead, I would regard their lines of argument as providing possible ways of viewing social phenomena and of justifying (giving arguments for) human behavior. We can, if we like, accept Freud's theory of infantile sexuality and thereby view the boy as loving his mother erotically and hating his father, whom he jealously sees as a suitor and competitor for his mother's affections. Freud's theory is interesting and illuminating insofar as it provides us with a different conception of people's behavior. It opens possibilities which we might otherwise have overlooked or not considered. Blum and McHugh (1971, p. 99) make a similar point with regard to Marx:

> [*T*]*he sociological import of economic determinism in Marx is not the impersonal effects of brute facts upon an organism, but rather his formulation of a meaningful environment constructed by and seen from the perspective of a typical actor. To say "economic determinism exists" is to decide to formulate actors as oriented to selected particular features of their socially organized environments in such a way as to enable this orientation (now called "the economy") to produce their routine actors. To describe economic determinism is then to assign a rule of relevance to actors which serves the purpose of explicating social structure by reference to their grounds of action (the economy) as a set of sociologically intelligible events of social structure (economic determinism).*

Freud and Marx, and their supporters and critics as well, consider their theories as more than just possible ways of thinking about the world and are, therefore, dependent upon the scientific community for deciding upon their truth or falsity. But we need not (although we may choose to) depend on research, empirical evidence, data, findings, or whatever for our acceptance of one or another explanation. We can view them as possibilities, ways to conceive of things, ways of trying to make sense of various social phenomena.

Consistent with this view of sociological inquiry, and far preferable to the dominant forms of explanation in sociology, are explanations which cite, appeal to, or ascribe pleasures, desires, motives, purposes, reasons, and the like as possible grounds for people's behavior. Behavior is thus described, explained, and evaluated by arguing that the situation *entitled* the actor or actors to act in a certain manner. This type of explanation is obviously different from seeking temporal antecedents (causes) or functional dependencies, as sociologists often do. For example, Lyman and Scott (1970, p. 3) emphasize the importance of "action," which "consists of the pursuit of ends by social actors capable of deliberating about the line of activity they undertake and of choosing among alternatives to the same end." They focus heavily on the significance of *talk,* stating (p. 3) that "men are capable of giving an account of their actions either as practically mental images of the action, its consequences and meanings, or as post hoc retrospective readings of completed acts. As images either before or after completion, these constructives emerge as statements made by the actor which give meaning to his actions." By *accounts,* they refer to statements "made by a social actor to explain unanticipated or untoward behavior—whether that behavior is his own or that of others, and whether the proximate cause for the statement arises from the actor himself or someone else. An account is not called for when people engage in routine, common-sense behavior in a cultural environment that recognizes that behavior as such" (p. 112). While I see no compelling reason why the notion of accounts should be restricted to only "unanticipated or untoward" behavior, I agree with Lyman and Scott that actors' accounts are frequently an important element in sociological inquiry.

Often, however, motives, reasons, and so on are ascribed by other actors and by the sociological inquirer: the analytic status of motives, reasons, and the like resides entirely in the actor's or inquirer's ascription and not in their concrete existence. Such a mode of explanation does not entirely restrict our employing the notion of "cause," although we must do so in a clearly limited manner.

Imagine a situation where Mrs. Jones' husband has behaved toward her in an abusive and violent manner over a period of several years. Finally, after he has pushed her down a flight of stairs, Mrs. Jones obtains a knife and kills her husband. We might want to say that this situation fits a typical formula of causal ascription: no B without A. Had he not been so violent and abusive, had he not pushed her down the stairs, she would not have killed him. However, to support such a causal assertion it is also necessary to show that, if A is not present, B will not occur, or that whenever A occurs B will follow. But B could conceivably occur without A; Mrs. Jones could have killed her husband for a great variety of reasons: he beat the children, or insulted her mother, or snored too loudly. And there are too many abusive and violent husbands for us to say with any degree of certainty that their behavior will always be followed by their wives' killing them. So concepts such as motive, reason, and purpose have a doubtful and indeterminate application. They lack the degree of certainty demanded by those who rely on causal explanations and should not be confused with such modes of analysis.

If we, as sociologists, accept responsibility for our own acts, our own thoughts, our own ideas, then we obviously do not regard them as necessitated. And if we exempt ourselves (quite properly, in my view) from the influence of deterministic forces, then how can we justify seeing the subjects of our inquiries as influenced by causal necessity? The answer, as I have tried to indicate, is that we cannot. All men offer reasons for their own and other people's actions, and this is what the sociologist does in his inquiries. In emphasizing the relevance of reasons, however, I do not wish to deny that there are many complexities and difficulties surrounding this form of explanation—although I will not consider them here. But for those dissatisfied with the usual emphasis on causal modes of analysis, much may be gained from seriously considering the writings of several philosophers who have devoted attention to reasons, purposes, and the like. Among them, the work of Toulmin (1970b), Peters (1958), Taylor (1964), and Louch (1969) are especially recommended.

As I pointed out in Chapter Eight, Max Weber believed that support for sociological theory should be based on the discovery of statistical laws or regularities, and most sociologists still hold the same view: the correctness of an interpretation depends on demonstration. However, we need not accept that approach, for we can regard such inquiries as Weber's concerning Protestantism and the rise of capitalism not as a process of discovery but as an assessment of arguments. From this viewpoint, the concern is with trying to show logical connections between certain situations and the behavior which these situations can be seen as entitling. Weber's thesis regarding religion and capitalism, then, can be seen as an attempt to present possible features of the situation as justifying or providing grounds for certain forms of behavior. The relationships, the connections which he discusses are not empirical but logical. Peter Winch advances this position in his excellent book *The Idea of a Social Science* and emphasizes the extent to which many sociological questions are to be "settled by *a priori* conceptual analysis rather than by empirical research" (1958, p. 17). What is needed, he notes, is not statistics or empirical research, but a better interpretation —not something different in kind.

While I am in general agreement with Winch's remarks, I find that he has little to say about what kinds of preparation or experiences are necessary or desirable for formulating various arguments about social life. He states, for instance, (pp. 134–135): "Whereas in natural science it is your theoretical knowledge which enables you to explain occurrences you have not previously met, a knowledge of logical theory on the other hand will not enable you to understand a piece of reasoning in an unknown language; you will have to learn that language, and that in itself *may* suffice to enable you to grasp the connections between the various parts of arguments in that language." If I understand Winch correctly, he is pointing out that to understand various sociological phenomena we must understand the language in which they are discussed, but that this may not be enough. We may also need to have some familiarity with the phenomena to which one or another argument is intended to apply. We need to understand what "counts" as a social phenomenon; what counts as anger, voting, or mental illness. Only someone who has learned how the silent movement of some-one's lips can serve as "worshipping God" will be in a position to recognize how the words "I'm praying" can serve to answer the question "Why are you moving your lips like that?" In short, we need to understand the form of life of those whose behavior concerns us.

But again we might ask: how are we to obtain such understanding? Obviously we cannot have direct experience in all human communities. As I have emphasized elsewhere (Phillips, 1971) sociologists seem generally unwilling to consider much of their experience as a possible source of understanding. They fail to consider what it "means" to be a husband, to have been a soldier, to have worked in a factory. Furthermore, many opportunities for experiencing the unexpected—playful activity, reading novels and history, studying philosophy or art, going to the theatre or the movies—are viewed as simply irrelevant or as impediments to doing sociology. Many sociologists seem so busy learning the proper methods, acquiring information, pursuing degrees, and doing research that it never occurs to them that some intimate familiarity with other social worlds might be necessary or at least desirable. It seems to me that those whose experience with mankind is increased are better able to consider alternative possibilities and to formulate certain judgments that are firmly anchored in their own experiences. Wittgenstein's remarks (1958, p. 227) concerning judgments about the genuineness of expressions are relevant here: "Corrector progress will generally issue from the judgments of those with better knowledge of mankind. Can one learn this knowledge? Yes; some can. Not, however, by taking a course in it, but through *'experience.'* Can someone else be a man's teacher in this? Certainly. From time to time he gives him a right *tip*. This is what 'learning' and 'teaching' are like here. What one acquires here is not a technique; one learns correct judgments. There are also rules, but they do not form a system, and only experienced people can apply them right. Unlike calculating-rules."

My discussion of argumentation has thus far been directed

at one aspect: that concerned with offering explanations for social phenomena. Let me now consider argumentation and related issues as they pertain to the sociologist's relations with an audience. I have already acknowledged that one cannot write without some sort of audience in mind, and I have suggested that we might try to direct our arguments to an audience larger than or different from that constituted by the community of sociologists—thus, hopefully, minimizing the extent to which we are bound by method. In presenting his arguments, the writer depends not so much on correct method as on providing *reasons* for his judgments. Whereas his explanation of the behavior of those he is writing about involves his attributing certain reasons (motives, purposes, and so on) to *them,* in his presentation to an audience he has to claim certain reasons for *himself* as supporting his explanations. Obviously, all argumentation assumes a means of communication, a common language. Beyond that, all arguments rely on certain commonsense, taken-for-granted theses, which will frequently be understood by the audience to whom he directs himself. When one writes about social phenomena, he assumes, for instance, that the audience considers this to be a proper subject for study, that they grant that people act for reasons, and that one can offer various explanations which make more or less sense, depending on the extent to which the writer and his audience share certain presuppositions, prejudices, and experiences. It is difficult to say exactly what is meant by "making sense." If I write "xayvrv," or "people are elephants," or "the reason he did it was because his teeth itched," such scribblings are unlikely to make any sense to my audience—or at least not to those with whom I wish to communicate. Whereas reliance on correct method supposedly allows the writer to set forth statements whose meaning should not give rise to argument, an emphasis on rhetoric and argumentation recognizes that this is impossible and that there is always room for misunderstanding or disagreement.

A crucial distinction between demonstration and argumentation is that the former relies on an epistemological position which holds truth to be something that can be directly and immediately attained, while the latter sees truth entirely as a social construction, as something resulting (if at all) from the confrontation of *opinions.* For those who emphasize method and demonstration, opinion is only mock truth; whereas from my position opinion is, in the strongest sense, that which has survived a variety of objections and criticisms. It is something in which we have a certain confidence—though not certainty, as with most notions of truth. Therefore, in setting forth reasons for this or that, one attempts to show how certain circumstances could entitle us to advance a certain opinion, a way of viewing things, a possibility. Such reasons, however, are not thought to be compelling, as are the products of reliance on method. While such notions as truth, objectivity, and reality aim at achieving certainty, opinion is directed at opening debate and creating confrontation. Perelman devotes considerable attention to the issue of argumentation, and much of my formulation here is based on his provocative writings. His views concerning the abandonment of a method of proof based on self-evidence are equally applicable to rejecting other methods (1963, p. 124): "But in default of an impersonal and absolute criterion of validity . . . we can still justify our decisions in the field of action and thought by forms of argument which are neither constraining nor mechanical. The guarantee of these, in the last analysis, is supplied by the solidarity which their use and their evaluation establishes between the person who constructs them and the person who adopts them. The responsibility of the man who thus engages himself is, as ever, a corollary of his freedom."

Of course, Perelman does not offer, nor can I, a list of the ingredients of a convincing argument. Were it possible to do so, to specify what a convincing form of argumentation would look like, we would only be trading the restrictions of one method for another. This is, in a sense, one of the strengths of an emphasis on argumentation: it allows us the freedom to utilize a multiplicity of rhetorical procedures to gain assent for our own point of view. Often we will fail, and other times a demagogue or a propagandist may use these rhetorical devices. But so may the genius, the saint, and the sage.

If nothing else, a general skepticism toward, if not an abandonment of, method should help us to recognize that man can be imprisoned as well liberated by the methods of science. It seems clear that science today occupies the sacred place once held by religion. And the social sciences especially can enslave us or they can perhaps help us to be reflective and self-conscious about our lives and our work. All that I have tried to do here is remind the reader that our methods are not gifts from the gods. The methods are our own construction and we need not accept them uncritically; in fact, we need not accept them at all. Let us abandon method, let us take ourselves and our own lives more seriously. George Orwell (1954, p. 177) once wrote: "Political language . . . is designed to make lies sound truthful and murder respectable and to give an appearance of solidity to pure wind." Perhaps this is a fitting epitaph to the eventual death of sociological method: *it gave an appearance of solidity to pure wind.*

Bibliography

ABEL, T. "The Operation Called *Verstehen.*" *American Journal of Sociology,* 1948, *54,* 211–218.

ABRAMSON, J. H. "Emotional Disorder, Status Inconsistency, and Migration." *Milbank Memorial Quarterly,* 1966, *44,* 23–48.

AJZEN, I., AND OTHERS. "Looking Backward Revisited: A Reply to Deutscher." *American Sociologist,* 1970, *5,* 267–273.

BAILEY, M. B., AND OTHERS. "The Epidemiology of Alcoholism in an Urban Residential Area." *Quarterly Journal of Studies on Alcohol,* 1965, *26,* 19–40.

BECKER, H. S. "Problems of Inference and Proof in Participant Observation." *American Sociological Review,* 1958, *23,* 652–660.

BECKER, H. S. "Whose Side Are We on? *Social Problems,* 1967, *14,* 239–247.

BELL, C. G., AND BUCHANAN, W. "Reliable and Unreliable Respondents: Party Registration and Prestige Pressure." *Western Political Quarterly,* 1956, *29,* 37–43.

BERELSON, B., AND STEINER, G. A. *Human Behavior: An Inventory of Scientific Findings.* New York: Harcourt, Brace & World, 1964.

BERGER, P. L. *Invitation to Sociology: A Humanistic Approach.* New York: Doubleday Anchor, 1963.

BIERSTEDT, R. *The Social Order: An Introduction to Sociology.* New York: McGraw-Hill, 1963.

BIERSTEDT, R. "Sociology and General Education." In C. H. Page (Ed.), *Sociology and Contemporary Education.* New York: Random House, 1964.

BINDER, A., AND OTHERS. "Verbal Conditioning as a Function of Experimenter Characteristics." *Journal of Abnormal Social Psychology,* Nov. 1957, *55,* 309–314.

BIRDWHISTELL, R. L. *Kinesics and Context: Essays on Body Motion Communication.* Philadelphia: University of Pennsylvania Press, 1970.

BLALOCK, H. M. *Causal Inferences in Nonexperimental Research.* Chapel Hill: University of North Carolina Press, 1964.

BLALOCK, H. M. "Comment on Coleman's Paper." In R. Bierstedt (Ed.), *A Design for Sociology: Scope, Objectives and Methods.* Philadelphia: The American Academy of Political and Social Science, 1969.

BLALOCK, H. M., AND BLALOCK, A. B. (Eds.) *Methodology in Social Research.* New York: McGraw-Hill, 1968.

BLOCK, J. *The Challenge of Response Sets.* New York: Meredith, 1965.

BLUM, A. F. "The Right Conduct of Sociology." Unpublished paper, 1970a.

BLUM, A. F. "Theorizing." In J. D. Douglas (Ed.), *Understanding Everyday Life.* Chicago: Aldine, 1970b.

BLUM, A. F., AND MC HUGH, P. "The Social Ascription of Motives." *American Sociological Review,* 1971, *36,* 98–109.

BLUMER, H. "What Is Wrong with Social Theory? *American Sociological Review,* 1954, *19,* 3–10.

BLUMER, H. "Sociological Analysis and the 'Variable.'" *American Sociological Review,* 1956, *21,* 683–690.

BLUMER, H. "Sociological Implications of the Thought of George Herbert Mead." *American Journal of Sociology,* 1966, *71,* 535–544.

BONJEAN, C. M., HALL, R. J. AND MC LEMORE, S. D. *Sociological Measurement.* San Francisco: Chandler, 1967.

BRADBURN, N. M. *The Structure of Psychological Well-Being.* Chicago: Aldine, 1969.

BRADBURN, N. M., AND CAPLOVITZ, D. *Reports on Happiness.* Chicago: Aldine, 1965.

BRAITHWAITE, R. B. *Scientific Explanation.* Cambridge, Mass.: Cambridge University Press, 1953.

BRESSLER, M. "Sociology and Collegiate General Education." In P. F. Lazarsfeld and others (Eds.), *The Uses of Sociology.* New York: Basic Books, 1967.

BRODBECK, M. (Ed.) *Readings in the Philosophy of the Social Sciences.* New York: Macmillan, 1959.

BROWN, J., AND GILMARTIN, B. G. "Sociology Today: Lacunae, Emphases and Surfeits." *American Sociologist,* 1969, *4,* 283–291.

BURTT, E. A. *The Metaphysical Foundations of Modern Science.* Garden City, N.Y.: Doubleday, 1954.

CAHALAN, D. "Correlates of Respondent Accuracy in the Denver Validity Survey." *Public Opinion Quarterly,* 1968, *32* (Winter), 607–621.

CAMPBELL, D. T., AND FISKE, D. W. "Convergent and Discriminant Validation by the Multitrait-Multimethod Matrix." *Psychological Bulletin,* 1959, *56,* 81–105.

CANNELL, C. F., AND FOWLER, F. J. "Comparison of a Self-Enumerative Procedure and a Personal Interview: A Validity Study." *Public Opinion Quarterly,* 1963, *27,* 250–264.

CANNELL, C. F., AND KAHN, R. L. "Interviewing." In G. Lindzey and E. Aronson (Eds.), *Handbook of Social Psychology.* Vol. II Reading, Mass.: Addison-Wesley, 1968.

CARR, E. H. *Michael Bakunin.* London: Macmillan, 1937.

CHRISTIE, R. "Authoritarianism Re-examined." In Richard Christie and M. Jahoda (Eds.), *Studies in the Scope and Method of "The Authoritarian Personality."* Glencoe, Ill.: Free Press, 1954.

CICOUREL, A. V. *Method and Measurement in Sociology.* New York: Free Press, 1964.

CLANCY, K. J. "Systematic Bias in Field Studies of Mental Illness." Unpublished doctoral dissertation. New York University, 1971.

CLANCY, K. J. AND GARSEN, R. "Why Some Attitude Scales Predict Better." *Journal of Advertising Research,* Oct. 1970, *10,* 33–38.

CLARK, E. L. "The Value of Student Interviewers." *Journal of Personal Research,* 1927, *5,* 204–207.

CLARK, J. P., AND TIFFT, L. L. "Polygraph and Interview Validation of Self-reported Deviant Behavior." *American Sociological Review,* Aug. 1966, *31,* 516–523.

CLARK, R. E. "The Relationship of Schizophrenia to Occupational Income and Occupational Prestige." *American Sociological Review,* 1948, *13,* 325–330.

CLAUSEN, A. "Response Validity: Vote Report." *Public Opinion Quarterly,* 1968, *32* (Winter), 588–606.

CLAUSEN, J. AND KOHN, M. L. "Relationship of Schizophrenia to Social Structure in a Small City." In B. Pasamanick (Ed.), *Epidemiology of Mental Disorder.* Washington, D.C.: American Association for the Advancement of Science, 1959.

CLOWARD, R., AND OHLIN, L. *Delinquency and Opportunity Structure.* Glencoe, Ill.: Free Press, 1960.

COLEMAN, J. S. "The Methods of Sociology." In R. Bierstedt (Ed.), *A Design for Sociology: Scope, Objectives, and Methods.* Philadelphia: The American Academy of Political and Social Science, 1969.

COLOMBOTOS, J. "The Effects of Personal vs. Telephone Interviews on Socially Acceptable Responses." Paper presented at the annual meeting of the American Society for Public Opinion Research, Groton, Connecticut, 1965.

COLOMBOTOS, J. "Personal vs. Telephone Interviews: Effect on Responses." Public Health Report, Sept. 1969, *84,* 773–782.

COOK, S., AND SELLITZ, C. "A Multiple Indicator Approach to Attitude Measurement." *Psychological Bulletin,* 1964, *62,* 36–55.

COSTNER, H. J. "Criteria for Measures of Association." *American Sociological Review,* 1965, *30,* 341–352.

COUCH, A. AND KENISTON, K. "Yeasayers and Naysayers: Agreeing Response Set as a Personality Variable." *Journal of Abnormal and Social Psychology,* March 1960, *60,* 151–174.

COWEN, E., AND TONGAS, P. "The Social Desirability of Trait Descriptive Terms." *Journal of Consulting Psychology,* 1959, *23,* 361–365.

CROWNE, D. AND MARLOWE, D. "A New Scale of Social Desirability Independent of Psycho-Pathology." *Journal of Consulting Psychology,* 1960, *24,* 349–354.

CROWNE, D., AND MARLOWE, D. *The Approval Motive.* New York: Wiley, 1964.

DAMARIN, F., AND MESSICK, S. "Response Styles as Personality Variables." *Research Bulletin, No. 65–10.* Princeton, N.J.: Educational Testing Service, 1965.

DENTLER, R. A., AND MONROE, L. J. "Early Adolescent Theft." *American Sociological Review,* Oct. 1961, *26,* 733–773.

DENZIN, N. K. *The Research Act.* Chicago: Aldine, 1970.

DEUTSCHER, I. "Words and Deeds; Social Science and Social Policy." *Social Problems,* 1966, *13,* 235–254.

DEUTSCHER, I. "Looking Backward: Case Studies on the Progress of Methodology in Sociological Research." *American Sociologist,* 1969, *4,* 35–41.

DI RENZO, G. J. (Ed.) *Concepts, Theory and Explanation in the Behavioral Sciences.* New York: Random House, 1966.

DOBY, J. T. "Logic and Levels of Scientific Explanation." In E. F. Borgatta and G. W. Bohrnstedt (Ed.), *Sociological Methodology. 1969.* San Francisco: Jossey-Bass, 1969.

DOHRENWEND, B., AND OTHERS. "Social Distance and Interviewer Effects." *Public Opinion Quarterly,* 1968, *31,* 410–422.

DOHRENWEND, B. P. "Social Status and Psychiatric Disorder: An Issue of Substance and an Issue of Method." *American Sociological Review,* Feb. 1966, *31,* 14–34.

DOHRENWEND, B. P., AND CRANDELL, D. L. "Some Relations among Psychiatric Symptoms, Organic Illness, and Social Class." *American Journal of Psychiatry,* 1967, *3,* 1527–1538.

DOHRENWEND, B. P., AND DOHRENWEND, B. "The Problem of Validity in Field Studies of Psychological Disorder." *International Journal of Psychiatry,* Oct. 1965, *1,* 585–610.

DOHRENWEND, B. P., AND DOHRENWEND, B. *Social Status and Psychological Disorder.* New York: Wiley, 1969.

DOUGLAS, J. D. *The Social Meaning of Suicide.* Princeton, N.J.: Princeton University Press, 1967.

DOUGLAS, J. D. (Ed.) *The Impact of Sociology.* New York: Appleton-Century-Crofts, 1970a.

DOUGLAS, J. D. (Ed.) *The Relevance of Sociology.* New York: Appleton-Century-Crofts, 1970b.

DUNHAM, H. W. *Community and Schizophrenia.* Detroit: Wayne State University Press, 1965.

DUNNETTE, M. D. "Fads, Fashions, and Folderol in Psychology." *American Psychologist,* 1966, *21,* 343–352.

DURKHEIM, E. *The Elementary Forms of Religious Life.* London: George Allen & Unwin, 1915.

DURKHEIM, E. *The Rules of Sociological Method.* New York: Free Press, 1938.

DURKHEIM, E. *The Division of Labor in Society.* Glencoe, Ill.: Free Press, 1949.

EDWARDS, A. "The Relationship Between the Judged Desirability of a Trait and the Probability That the Trait Will Be Endorsed." *Journal of Applied Psychology,* 1953, *37,* 90–93.

EDWARDS, A. *The Social Desirability Variable in Personality Assessment and Research.* New York: Dryden Press, 1957.

EDWARDS, A. "Social Desirability and Personality Test Construction." In B. M. Bass and I. A. Berg (Eds.), *Objective Approaches to Personality.* New York, Van Nostrand, 1959.

EDWARDS, A., AND OTHERS. "Response Sets and Factor Loadings on 61 Personality Scales." *Journal of Applied Psychology,* 1962, *46,* 220–225.

EHRLICH, J., AND RIESMAN, D. "Age and Authority in the Interview." *Public Opinion Quarterly,* 1961, *23,* 39–56.

EMMET, D., AND MAC INTYRE, A. *Sociological Theory and Philosophical Analysis.* London: Macmillan, 1970.

ERICKSON, M., AND EMPEY, L. "Court Records: Undetected Delinquency and Decision Making." *Journal of Criminal Law.* Dec. 1963, *54,* 458–469.

FESTINGER, L. "Laboratory Experiments." In L. Festinger and D. Katz (Eds.), *Research Methods in the Behavioral Sciences.* New York: Dryden Press, 1953.

FEYERABEND, P. K. "Against Method: Outline of an Anarchistic Theory of Knowledge." *Minnesota Studies in the Philosophy of Science,* 1970, *4,* 17–130.

FEYERABEND, P. K. "Consolations for the Specialist." In I. Lakatos and A. Musgrave (Eds.), *Criticism and the Growth of Knowledge.* Cambridge, Mass.: Cambridge University Press.

FILMER, P., PHILLIPSON, M., SILVERMAN, D., AND WALSH, D. *New Directions in Sociological Theory.* London: Collier-Macmillan, 1972.

FRIEDSON, E. L. *Profession of Medicine.* New York: Dodd, Mead, 1970.

FREUD, S. *Collected Papers.* Vol. 4. New York: Basic Books, 1959.

FRIEDMAN, N. *The Social Nature of Psychological Research.* New York: Basic Books, 1967.

FRIEDRICHS, R. W. *A Sociology of Sociology.* New York: Free Press, 1970.

FRUMKIN, R. M. "Occupation and Mental Illness." *Public Welfare Statistics,* 1952, *7,* 4–13.

GADOUREK, I. "Derek L. Phillips' Research to End the Research." *Mens en Maatschappij,* 1972, *47,* 119–128.

GAMBERG, H. "Science and Scientism: The State of Sociology." *American Sociologist,* 1969, *4,* 111–116.

GARFINKEL, H. "Commonsense Knowledge of Social Structures: The Documentary Method of Interpretation in Lay and Professional

Fact Finding." In J. M. Scher (Eds.), *Theories of the Mind.* New York: Free Press, 1962.

GARFINKEL, H. "Studies of the Routine Grounds of Everyday Activities." *Social Problems,* 1964, *11,* 225–250.

GARFINKEL, H. *Studies in Ethnomethodology.* Englewood Cliffs, N.J.: Prentice-Hall, 1967.

GARFINKEL, H. "Social Science Evidence and the School Segregation Cases." In J. D. Douglas (Ed.), *The Impact of Sociology.* New York: Appleton-Century-Crofts, 1970.

GOFFMAN, E. *Encounters.* Indianapolis, Ind.: Bobbs-Merrill, 1961.

GOULDNER, A. W. "Anti-Minotaur: The Myth of a Value-Free Sociology." *Social Problems,* 1962, *9,* 199–213.

GOULDNER, A. W. "The Sociologist as Partisan: Sociology and the Welfare State." *American Sociologist,* 1968, *3* 103–166.

GOULDNER, A. W. *The Coming Crisis of Western Sociology.* New York: Basic Books, 1970.

GOULDNER, A. W. "The Politics of the Mind." *Social Policy,* 1972, *2,* 15–30.

GRAHAM, S. R. "The Influence of Therapist Character Structure upon Rorschach Changes in the Course of Psychotheropy." *American Psychologist,* 1960, *15,* 415–416.

GREEN, L. W. "East Pakistan: Knowledge and Use of Contraceptives." *Studies in Family Planning,* 1969, *39,* 9–14.

GURIN, G., VEROFF, J. AND FELD, S. *Americans View Their Mental Health.* New York: Basic Books, 1960.

HABERMAN, P. W. "The Use of a Psychological Test for Recall of Past Situations." *Journal of Clinical Psychology,* 1963, *19,* 245–248.

HABERMAS, J. *Knowledge and Human Interests.* Boston: Beacon Press, 1971.

HAMBLIN, R. L. "Ratio Measurement and Sociological Theory." Department of Sociology, Washington University, St. Louis, 1966. Mimeographed.

HAMBRIGHT, T. Z. "Comparisons of Information on Death Certificates and Matching 1960 Census Records: Age, Marital Status, Race, Nativity, and Country of Origin." *Demography,* 1969, *6,* 413–423.

HAMPSHIRE, S. "Identification and Existence." In H. D. Lewis (Ed.), *Contemporary British Philosophy, Third Series.* New York: Macmillan, 1956.

HANSON, N. R. *Patterns of Discovery.* Cambridge, Mass.: Cambridge University Press, 1958.

HARRE, R. *Matter and Method.* New York: Macmillan, 1964.

HAUSER, P. "Comments on Coleman's Paper." In R. Bierstedt (Ed), *Design for Sociology: Scope, Objectives, and Methods.* Philadelphia: The American Academy of Political and Social Science, 1969.

HEILBRUN, A. B. "Social Learning Theory, Social Desirability and the MMPI." *Psychological Bulletin,* May 1964, *61,* 377–387.

HEISE, D. "Problems in Path Analysis and Causal Inference." In E. Borgatta and G. W. Bohrnstedt (Eds.), *Sociological Methodology 1969* San Francisco: Jossey-Bass, 1969.

HEMPEL, C. G., AND OPPENHEIM, K. "Theory of Scientific Explanation." In H. Feigel and M. Brodbeck (Eds.), *Readings in the Philosophy of Science.* New York: Macmillan, 1953.

HERMANS, H. J. M. "The Influence of Situation and Condition on the Responses to Questionnaires." *Sociologia Neerlandica,* 1970, *VI,* 1–11.

HINDELANG, M. J. "Age, Sex, and the Versatility of Delinquent Involvements." *Social Problems,* 1971, *18,* 522–535.

HOLLINGSHEAD, A. B., AND REDLICH, F. C. *Social Class and Mental Illness.* New York: Wiley, 1958.

HOROWITZ, I. L. *Professing Sociology: Studies in the Life Cycle of Social Science.* Chicago: Aldine, 1968.

HUGHES, H. S. *Consciousness and Society.* New York: Vintage, 1961.

HUIZINGA, J. *Homo Ludens.* Boston: Beacon, 1962.

HYMAN, H. *Interviewing in Social Research.* Chicago: University of Chicago Press, 1954.

HYMAN, H. *Survey Design and Analysis.* Glencoe, Ill.: Free Press, 1955.

HYMES, D. "Introduction: Toward Ethnographies of Communication." *American Anthropologist,* 1964, *66,* 1–25.

KAPLAN, B., REED, R. B., AND RICHARDSON, W. "A Comparison of the Incidence of Hospitalized and Non-hospitalized Cases of Psychosis in Two Communities." *American Sociological Review,* 1956, *21,* 472–479.

KAUFMAN, F. *Methodology of the Social Sciences.* New York: Humanities Press, 1958.

KIRSCHT, J. P., AND DILLEHAY, R. C. *Dimensions of Authoritarianism: A Review of Theory and Research.* Lexington: University of Kentucky Press, 1967.

KOLAKOWSKI, L. *Positivist Philosophy.* Harmondsworth, Eng.: Pelican Books, 1972.

KORNHAUSER, W. *The Politics of Mass Society.* Glencoe, Ill.: Free Press, 1959.

KUHN, T. S. *The Structure of Scientific Revolutions.* Chicago: University of Chicago Press, 1962.

KUHN, T. S. *The Structure of Scientific Revolutions.* Second edition. Chicago: University of Chicago Press, 1970a.

KUHN, T. S. "Reflections on My Critics." In I. Lakatos and A. Musgrave (Eds.), *Criticism and the Growth of Knowledge.* Cambridge, Mass.: Cambridge University Press, 1970b.

LABOWITZ, S., AND HAGEDORN, R. *Introduction to Social Research.* New York: McGraw-Hill, 1971.

LAKATOS, I. "Falsification and the Methodology of Scientific Research Programmes." In I. Lakatos and A. Musgrave (Eds.), *Criticism and the Growth of Knowledge.* Cambridge, Mass.: Cambridge University Press, 1970.

LAKATOS, I., AND MUSGRAVE, A. (Eds.) *Criticism and the Growth of Knowledge.* Cambridge, Mass.: Cambridge University Press, 1970.

LANGNER, T. "A Twenty-Two Item Screening Score of Psychiatric Symptoms Indicating Impairment." *Journal of Health and Human Behavior,* 1962, *3,* 269–276.

LANGNER, T. S. "Psycho-Physiological Symptoms and the Status of Women in Two Mexican Communities." In J. M. Murphy and A. H. Leighton (Eds.), *Approaches to Cross-Cultural Psychiatric.* Ithaca, N.Y.: Cornell University Press, 1965.

LAZARSFELD, P. F., SEWELL, W. H., AND WILENSKY, H. L. (Eds.) *The Uses of Sociology.* New York: Basic Books, 1967.

LEBERGOTT, S. "Labor Force and Employment Trends." In E. Shelden and W. E. Moore (Eds.), *Indicators of Social Change.* New York: Russell Sage, 1968.

LEIGHTON, D., AND OTHERS. *The Character of Danger.* New York: Basic Books, 1964.

LENSKI, G. E., AND LEGGETT, J. C. "Caste, Class and Deference in the Research Interview." *American Journal of Sociology,* 1960, *65,* 463–467.

LEWIS, O. *Life in a Mexican Village: Tepoztlan Restudied.* Urbana: University of Illinois Press, 1951.

LIPSET, S. M., AND LOWENTHAL, L. (Eds.) *Culture and Social Character.* New York: Free Press, 1961.

LODAHL, J., AND GORDON, G. "The Structure of Scientific Fields and the

Functioning of University Graduate Departments." *American Sociological Review,* 1972, *37,* 57–72.

LOUCH, A. R. *Explanation and Human Action.* Berkeley: University of California Press, 1969.

LYMAN, S. A., AND SCOTT, M. B. *A Sociology of the Absurd.* New York: Appleton-Century-Crofts, 1970.

LYND, R. S. *Knowledge for What?* New York: Grove Press, 1964.

LYND, S. "A Profession of History." *New American Review,* No. 2. New York: New American Library, 1968.

MACCOBY, E., AND MACCOBY, N. "The Interview: A Tool of Social Science." In G. Lindsey (Ed.), *Handbook of Social Psychology.* Vol. I. Reading, Mass.: Addison-Wesley, 1954

MC DILL, E. L. "Anomie, Authoritarianism, Prejudice, and Socioeconomic Status: An Attempt at Clarification." *Social Forces,* 1961, *39,* 239–245.

MC GUIRE, W. J. "Personality and Susceptibility to Social Influence." In E. F. Borgatta and W. W. Lambert (Eds.), *Handbook of Personality Theory and Research.* Chicago: Rand McNally, 1968.

MC GUIRE, W. J. "Suspiciousness of Experimenter's Intent." In R. Rosenthal and R. L. Rosnow (Eds.), *Artifact in Behavioral Research.* New York: Academic Press, 1969.

MC HUGH, P. "On the Failure of Positivism." In J. D. Douglas (Ed.), *Understanding Everyday Life.* Chicago: Aldine, 1970.

MC WILLIAMS, W. C. "Political Arts and Political Sciences." In P. Green and S. Levinson (Eds.), *Power and Community.* New York: Vintage Books, 1970.

MANIS, J., BRAWER, M. J., HUNT, C. L., AND KERCHER, L. C. "Validating a Mental Health Scale." *American Sociological Review,* Feb. 1963, *28,* 108–116.

MANIS, J. "Estimating the Prevalence of Mental Illness." *American Sociological Review,* Feb. 1964, *29,* 84–89.

MANNHEIM, K. *Ideology and Utopia.* New York: Harcourt, Brace & World, 1968.

MARTIN, H. W. "Mental Health of Eastern Oklahoma Indians." *Human Organization,* 1968, *27,* 308–315.

MARX, K., AND ENGELS, F. *The German Ideology.* Parts I and III. New York: International Publishers, 1947.

MASLOW, A., AND MINTZ, N. "Effects of Esthetic Surroundings: I. Initial Effects of Three Esthetic Conditions upon Perceiving 'Energy' and 'Well-Being' in Faces." *Journal of Psychology,* 1956, *41,* 247–254.

MASTERMAN, M. "The Nature of a Paradigm." In I. Lakatos and A. Musgrave (Eds.), *Criticism and the Growth of Knowledge.* Cambridge, Mass.: Cambridge University Press, 1970.

MATARAZZO, J. D., AND OTHERS. "Studies in Interview Speech Behavior." In L. Krasner and L. P. Ullman (Eds.), *Research in Behavior Modification.* New York: Holt, Rinehart & Winston, 1965.

MEILE, R., AND HAESE, P. "Social Status, Status Congruence, and Symptoms of Stress." *Journal of Health and Human Behavior,* 1969, *10,* 237–244.

MEEHAN, E. J. *Explanation in Social Science: A System Paradigm.* Homewood, Ill.: Dorsey, 1968.

MENZEL, H. "Public and Private Conformity under Different Conditions of Acceptance in the Group." *Journal of Abnormal and Social Psychology,* 1957, *55,* 398–402.

MENZEL, H., AND OTHERS. "Dimensions of Being 'Modern' in Medical Practice." *Journal of Chronic Diseases,* January–June 1959, *9,* 20–40.

MENZEL, H., AND KATZ, E. "Comments on Charles Winnick, 'the Diffusion of an Innovation Among Physicians in a Large City.'" *Sociometry,* 1963, *26,* 125–127.

MERTON, R. K. *Social Theory and Social Structure.* New York: Free Press, 1957.

MILLER, S. M., AND RIESSMAN, F. "Working Class Authoritarianism: A Critique of Lipset." *British Journal of Sociology,* 1961, *21,* 263–276.

MILLS, C. W. *The Sociological Imagination.* New York: Oxford University Press, 1959.

MINTZ, N. "Effects of Esthetic Surroundings: II. Prolonged and Repeated Experience in a 'Beautiful' and an 'Ugly' Room." *Journal of Psychology,* 1956, *41,* 459–466.

MITCHELL, R. E. "Some Social Implications of High Density Housing." *American Sociological Review,* 1971, *36,* 18–29.

MORGAN, C. *Introduction to Psychology.* New York: McGraw-Hill, 1956.

NETTLER, G. *Explanations.* New York: McGraw-Hill, 1970.

NICOLAUS, M. "Remarks at ASA Convention." *American Sociologist,* 1969, *4,* 154–156.

NIETZSCHE, F. In K. Schlechta (Ed.), *Werke in drei Bänden.* Vol. III. Munich: Carl Hanser, 1955.

NUNNALLY, J. *Psychometric Theory.* New York: McGraw-Hill, 1967.

NYE, I., AND SHORT, J. "Scaling Delinquent Behavior." *American Sociological Review,* June 1957, *22,* 326–331.

ORDEN, S. R., AND BRADBURN, N. M. "Dimensions of Marriage Happiness." *American Journal of Sociology,* 1968, *73,* 715–731.

ORDEN, S. R., AND BRADBURN, N. M. "Working Wives and Marriage Happiness." *American Journal of Sociology,* 1969, *74,* 392–402.

ORNE, M. T. "On the Social Psychology of the Psychological Experiment: With Particular Reference to Demand Characteristics and Their Implications." *American Psychologist,* 1962, *17,* 776–783.

ORNE, M. T. *"Demand Characteristics and the Concept of Quasi-Con*trols." In R. Rosenthal and R. L. Rosnow (Eds.), *Artifact in Behavioral Research,* New York: Academic Press, 1969.

ORWELL, G. *A Collection of Essays.* Garden City, N.Y.: Doubleday Anchor, 1954.

PALMER, R. E. *Hermeneutics.* Evanston, Ill.: Northwestern University Press, 1969.

PARRY, H., AND CROSSLEY, H. "Validity of Responses to Survey Questions." *Public Opinion Quarterly,* 1950, *14,* 61–80.

PARSONS, T. *The Structure of Social Action.* Glencoe, Ill.: Free Press, 1949.

PASAMANICK, B., ROBERTS, D. W., LEMKAU, P. W., AND KRUEGER, D. B. "A Survey of Mental Disease in an Urban Area: Prevalence by Race and Income." In B. Pasamanick, *Epidemiology of Disorder.* Washington, D. C.: American Association for the Advancement of Science, 1959.

PEIRCE, C. S. "How to Make Our Ideas Clear." In V. Tomes (Ed.), *Essays in the Philosophy of Science.* Indianapolis: Bobbs-Merrill, 1957.

PERELMAN, C. *The Idea of Justice and the Problem of Argument.* London: Routledge & Kegan Paul, 1963.

PETERS, R. S. *The Concept of Motivation.* London: Routledge & Kegan Paul, 1958.

PHILLIPS, D. L. "The 'True Prevalence' of Mental Illness in a New England State." *Community Mental Health Journal,* 1966, *2* (Spring), 35–40.

PHILLIPS, D. L. "Social Participation and Happiness." *American Journal of Sociology,* 1967, *72,* 479–488.

PHILLIPS, D. L. *Knowledge from What? Theories and Methods in Social Research.* Chicago: Rand McNally, 1971.

PHILLIPS, D., AND CLANCY, K. "Reply to Harvey." *American Sociological Review,* June 1971, *36,* 512–515.

PHILLIPS, D., AND SEGAL, B. "Sexual Status and Psychiatric Symptoms." *American Sociological Review,* Feb. 1969, *34,* 58–72.

PLANCK, M. *Scientific Autobiography and Other Papers.* Tr. by Frank Gaynor. New York: Philosophical Library, 1949.

PLATO. *The Collected Dialogues.* E. Hamilton and H. Cairns (Eds.) Princeton: Princeton University Press, 1969.

POLANYI, M. *Personal Knowledge: Towards a Post-Critical Philosophy.* New York: Harper and Row, 1958.

POPPER, K. R. *The Logic of Scientific Discovery.* New York: Basic Books, 1959.

POPPER, K. R. "Fact, Standards, and Truth: A Further Criticism of Relativism." Addendum I in K. Popper, *The Open Society and Its Enemies.* 4th Ed. Vol. II. New York: Harper and Row, 1961.

POPPER, K. R. *Conjectures and Refutations.* London: Routledge & Kegan Paul, 1963.

POPPER, K. R. "On the Theory of Objective Mind." *Proceedings of the XIV International Congress of Philosophy,* I: 25–53, 1968.

POPPER, K. R. "Epistemology Without a Knowing Subject." In J. H. Grill (Ed.), *Philosophy Today.* No. 2. New York: Macmillan, 1969.

PRICE, J. L. *Social Facts: Introductory Readings.* New York: Macmillan, 1969.

RAFFEL, S. "Notes on Authorship." Unpublished paper, 1970.

REDFIELD, R. *Tepoztlan: A Mexican Village.* Chicago: University of Chicago Press, 1930.

REGAN, W. "Basic and Applied Research: A Meaningful Distinction?" *Science,* 1967, *155,* 1383–1386.

REISS, A., AND RHODES, A. "The Distribution of Juvenile Delinquency in the Social Class Structure." *American Sociological Review,* Oct. 1961, *26,* 720–732.

REISS, I. *The Social Context of Premarital Permissiveness.* New York: Holt, Rinehart and Winston, 1967.

REYNOLDS, L. T., AND REYNOLDS, J. M. (Eds.) *The Sociology of Sociology.* New York: David McKay, 1970.

RICHARDSON, S., DOHRENWEND, B. S., AND KLEIN, D. *Interviewing: Its Forms and Functions.* New York: Basic Books, 1965.

RIECKEN, H. W. "A Program for Research on Experiments in Social

Psychology." In N. F. Washburn (Ed.), *Decisions, Values and Groups.* New York: Pergamon Press, 1962.

RILEY, M. W. *Sociological Research.* New York: Harcourt, Brace and World, 1963.

ROBERTS, A. H., AND ROKEACH, M. "Anomie, Authoritarianism, and Prejudice: A Replication." *American Journal of Sociology,* 1956, *61,* 355–358.

ROBINSON, J., AND ROHDE, S. "Two Experiments with an Anti-Semitism Poll." *Journal of Abnormal and Social Psychology,* 1946, *41,* 136–144.

ROBINSON, J. P., AND SHAVER, P. *Measures of Social Psychological Attitudes.* Ann Arbor, Mich.: Institute for Social Research, University of Michigan, 1969.

ROGERS, E. M., WITH SHOEMAKER, F. F. *Communication of Innovations.* New York: Free Press, 1971.

ROSEN, E. "Self-Appraisal, Personal Desirability and Perceived Social Desirability of Personality Traits." *Journal of Abnormal and Social Psychology,* 1956, *52,* 151–158.

ROSENBERG, M. J. "Images in Relation to the Policy Process: American Public Opinion on Cold War Issues." In H. C. Kelman (Ed.), *International Behavior: A Social Psychological Approach.* New York: Holt, Rinehart & Winston, 1965a.

ROSENBERG, M. J. "When Dissonance Fails: On Eliminating Evaluation Apprehension from Attitude Measurement." *Journal of Personality and Social Psychology,* 1965b, *1,* 18–42.

ROSENBERG, M. J. "Attitude Change and Foreign Policy in the Cold War Era." In J. N. Rosenau (Ed.), *Domestic Sources of Foreign Policy.* New York: Free Press, 1967.

ROSENBERG, M. J. "The Conditions and Consequences of Evaluation Apprehension." In R. Rosenthal and R. L. Rosnow (Eds.), *Artifact in Behavioral Research.* New York: Academic Press, 1969.

ROSENTHAL, R. *Experimenter Effects in Behavioral Research.* New York: Appleton-Century-Crofts, 1966.

ROSENTHAL, R., AND ROSNOW, R. L. *Artifact in Behavioral Research.* New York and London: Academic Press, 1969.

SAMPSON, E. E., AND FRENCH, J. R. F. "An Experiment on Active and Passive Resistance to Social Power." *American Psychologist,* 1960, *15,* 396.

SCHUTZ, A. "Concept and Theory Formation in the Social Sciences."

In D. Emmet and A. McIntyre (Eds.), *Sociological Theory and Philosophical Analysis*. London: Macmillan, 1970.

SEARS, R. R. "Social Behavior and Personality Development." In T. Parsons and E. A. Shils (Eds), *Toward a General Theory of Action*. Cambridge: Harvard University Press, 1951.

SECHREST, L. "Testing, Measuring, and Assessing People." In E. F. Borgatta and W. W. Lambert (Eds.), *Handbook of Personality Theory and Research*. Chicago: Rand McNally, 1968.

SELLTIZ, C., JAHODA, M., DEUTSCH, M., AND COOK, S. W. *Research Methods in Social Relations*. New York: Holt, Rinehart and Winston, 1963.

SIMMEL, G. *The Sociology of Georg Simmel*. Trans. and edited by K. H. Wolff. Glencoe, Ill.: Free Press, 1950.

SJOBERG, G., AND NETT, R. *A Methodology for Social Research*. New York: Harper & Row, 1968.

SKINNER, B. F. "Experimental Psychology." In W. Dennis (Ed.), *Current Trends in Psychology*. Pittsburgh: University of Pittsburgh Press, 1947.

SMELSER, N. J. *Essays in Sociological Explanation*. Englewood Cliffs, N.J.: Prentice-Hall, 1968.

SMELSER, N. J. "The Optimum Scope of Sociology." In R. Bierstedt (Ed.), *A Design for Sociology: Scope, Objectives, and Methods*. Philadelphia: American Academy of Political and Social Science, 1969.

SMELSER, N. J., AND DAVIS, J. A. *Sociology*. Englewood Cliffs, N.J.: Prentice-Hall, 1969.

SPITZER, S. P., AND DENZIN, N. K. "Levels of Knowledge in an Emergent Crisis." *Social Forces*, 1965, *44*, 234–237.

SROLE, L. "Social Integration and Certain Corollaries." *American Sociological Review*, Dec. 1956, *21*, 706–716.

SROLE, L., LANGNER, T. S., MICHAEL, S. T., OPLER, M. K., AND RENNIE, T. A. C. *Mental Health in the Metropolis*. New York: McGraw-Hill, 1962.

STEMBER, C. H. *Education and Attitude Change*. New York: Institute of Human Relations Press, 1961.

STINCHCOMBE, A. "Some Empirical Consequences of the Davis-Moore Theory of Stratification." In R. Bendix and S. M. Lipset (Eds.), *Class, Status and Power*. New York: Free Press, 1966.

STORER, N. W. *The Social System of Science*. New York: Harper, 1966.

STRAUSS, M. "Measuring Families." In H. Christensen (Ed.), *Hand-*

book of Marriage and the Family. Chicago: Rand McNally, 1964.

SUMMERS, G. F., AND HAMMONDS, A. D. "Toward a Paradigm for Respondent Bias in Survey Research." *Sociological Quarterly*, 1969, *39*, 113–121.

SUMMERS, G. F., AND OTHERS. "Psychiatric Symptoms: Cross-Validation with a Rural Sample." *Rural Sociology*, 1971, *36*, 367–378.

TAYLOR, C. *The Explanation of Behavior*. London: Routledge & Kegan Paul, 1964.

TILLY, C. "Letter to the Editor." *American Sociologist*, 1966, *1*, 84.

TOULMIN, S. *The Uses of Argument*. Cambridge, Mass.: Cambridge University Press, 1969.

TOULMIN, S. "Does the Distinction Between Normal and Revolutionary Science Hold Water?" In I. Lakatos and A. Musgrave (Eds.), *Criticism and the Growth of Knowledge*. Cambridge, Mass.: Cambridge University Press, 1970a.

TOULMIN, S. "Reasons and Causes." In R. Borger and F. Cioffi (Eds.), *Explanation in the Behavior Sciences*. Cambridge, Mass.: Cambridge University Press, 1970b.

TRAGER, G. L. "Paralanguage: A First Approximation." *Studies in Linguistics*, 1958, *13*, 1–12.

TRUMAN, D. "Disillusion and Regeneration: The Quest for a Discipline." *American Political Science Review*, Dec. 1965, 865–871.

TUMIN, M. M. "In Dispraise of Loyalty." *Social Problems*, 1968, *15*, 267–279.

TURNER, R. "Role-Taking: Process Vesus Conformity." In A. M. Rose (Ed.), *Human Behavior and Social Processes: An Interactionist Approach*. Boston: Houghton Mifflin, 1962.

TWIGG, J. "Collecting Research Data: What Is Interviewer Bias?" *The Advertising Quarterly*, 1969–1970, *22*, 9–16.

U. S. Bureau of the Census. *Evaluation and Research Program of the U. S. Census of Population and Housing, 1960: The Employer Record Check*. E.R. 60, No. 6, 1965.

WANKLIN, J. M., AND OTHERS. "Factors Influencing the Rate of First Admission to Mental Hospital." *Journal of Nervous and Mental Disease*, 1955, *121*, 103–116.

WEBB, E. J., CAMPBELL, D. T., SCHWARTZ, R. D., AND SECHREST, L. *Unobtrusive Measures: Non-Reactive Research*. Chicago: Rand McNally, 1966.

WEBER, M. *The Theory of Social and Economic Organization*. New York: Oxford University Press, 1947.

WEBER, M. *Basic Concepts in Sociology.* New York: Collier Books, 1963.

WEIGERT, A. J. "The Immoral Rhetoric of Scientific Sociology." *American Sociologist,* 1970, *5,* 111–120.

WEISS, C. "Validity of Welfare Mothers' Interview Responses." *Public Opinion Quarterly,* 1968, *32* (Winter), 622–633.

WELLS, W. "How Chronic Overclaimers Distort Survey Findings." *Journal of Advertising Research,* 1963, *3,* 8–18.

WHITEHEAD, A. N. *Adventures of Ideas.* New York: Macmillan, 1933.

WHYTE, W. F. "The Role of the U. S. Professor in Developing Countries." *American Sociologist,* 1969, *4,* 19–28.

WIGGINS, J., AND RUMRILL, C. "Social Desirability in the MMPI and Welsh's Factor Scales A and R." *Journal of Consulting Psychology,* 1959, *23,* 100–106.

WILLIAMS, J. A., JR. "Interviewer Role Performance: A Further Note on Bias in the Information Interview." *Public Opinion Quarterly,* 1968, *32,* 287–294.

WILSON, T. P. "Conceptions of Interaction and Forms of Sociological Explanation." *American Sociological Review,* 1970, *35,* 697–710.

WINCH, P. *The Idea of a Social Science.* New York: Humanities Press, 1958.

WINKEL, G., AND SARASON, I. "Subject, Experimenter, and Situational Variables in Research Anxiety." *Journal of Abnormal and Social Psychology,* 1964, *68,* 601–603.

WITTGENSTEIN, L. *Tractatus Logico-Philosophicus.* London: Kegan Paul, Trench, Trubner, 1922.

WITTGENSTEIN, L. *Philosophical Investigations.* New York: Macmillan, 1958.

WOLIN, S. S. *Politics and Vision.* Boston: Little, Brown, 1960.

ZETTERBERG, H. *On Theory and Verification in Sociology.* Totowa, N.J.: Bedminster Press, 1966.

ZIMAN, J. *Public Knowledge: The Social Dimension of Science.* Cambridge, Mass.: Cambridge University Press, 1968.

★★★★★★★★★★★★★★★★

Index

★★★★★★★★★★★★★★★★